One Rembrandt for Twenty-Five Jews

Robert Lemm

One Rembrandt for Twenty-Five Jews

Hemann Göring's present for Hilter

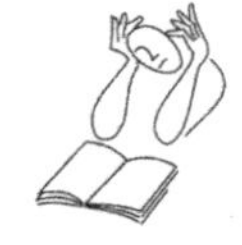

Aspekt Publishers

One Rembrandt for Twenty-Five Jews

Amersfoortsestraat 27, 3769 AD Soesterberg, The Netherlands
info@uitgeverijaspekt.nl – http://www.uitgeverijaspekt.nl

Cover: Maarten Bakker
Inside: Thomas Wunderink

ISBN: 9789461539427
NUR: 680

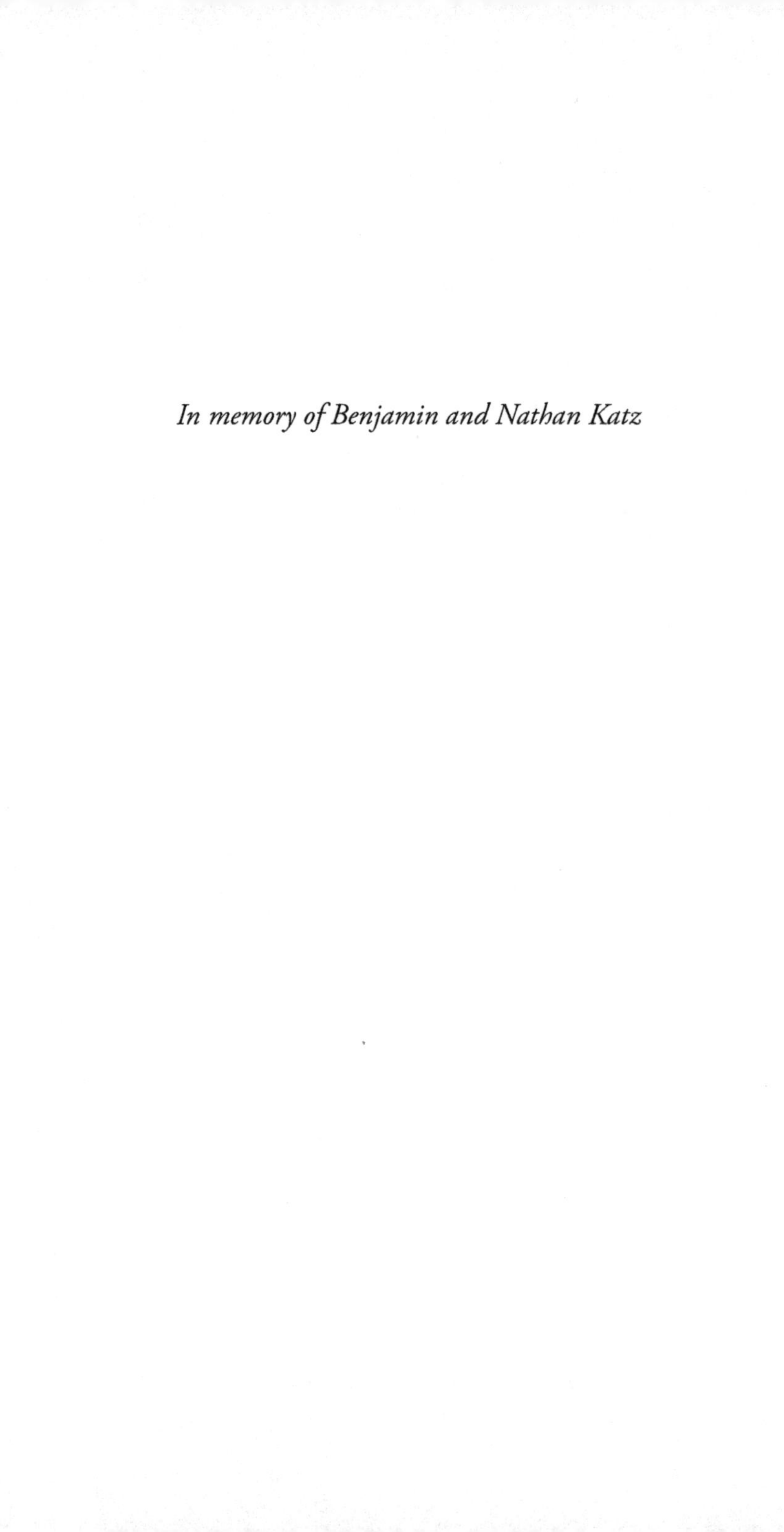

In memory of Benjamin and Nathan Katz

Contents

Preface

During the final years of the nineties I met David Cohen, shortly after, for the Steven Spielberg project, more than fifty thousand stories were recorded about the Holocaust survivors. David and his wife Stephanie Weinbaum had participated. And the remarkable fact was that, until then, for half a century, they had kept their stories to themselves. They didn't even tell their children. Why they, and in particularly David had kept quiet for so long, will be unfold in the subsequent pages.

Some of the facts weren't completely unknown. In the standard reference work *Het Koninkrijk der Nederlanden in de Tweede Wereldoorlog* written by Dr. Lou de Jong, Part 5 from 1974, one can read the following: 'Other than before the 23th of October 1941, practically no Jew was given an *Ausreisevisum (Exit Visa)* if they weren't able to pay, themselves or via relations abroad, the Third Reich a considerable amount of money in foreign currency. Approximately one hundred and twenty Jews were able to leave the Netherlands between 23 October 1942 and the end of 1942 by handing over this amount of money. Sometimes one would have to give 100.000 Swiss francs per family, in a few cases even half a million. The Dutch Foreign Exchange Institute had supplied three million of those francs, which wealthy Jews could buy for an applicable rate (however, this rate varied) in exchange for that coveted document: an *Ausreisevisum (Exit Visa)*. Art dealers and brothers

Benjamin and Nathan Katz from Dieren acquired this document because they, after having been employed at the, to be established, *Führermuseum* in Linz, offered up a valuable collection of etchings and drawings to that museum. Rauter, Germany's highest representative of the SS in the Netherlands, wanted to keep a hold of them, but Goering, Hitler's Reichsmarschall, who had profited from their work, got what he wanted, and in the end it was Lages himself, German Chief in Holland of the Center for Jewish Emigration, who guided the Katz brothers to the Spanish border; their eighty-three year old mother was allowed to remain in Dieren without having to wear a yellow badge.'

Some details in the above mentioned words are not true, but, in short, here we have the first official report of the events that actually took place and that are revealed in this book.

David Cohen was one of the Katz brothers' nephews and ten years old at the time of the *Ausreisevisum (Exit Visa).* He was one of the brothers' twenty-five family members who, thanks to that visa, was able to leave the Netherlands. In order to honor his uncles he decided to write down his story. Shortly after his participation in the Spielberg project he asked me for help. However, it still took more than a decade before our cooperation bore fruit. David had just turned eighty years old and his memories needed time to reconstruct certain passages and verify the facts. Situations surfaced that required further explanation, and there were gaps that needed to be filled. In the end we finished a book that does justice to the experiences of a man who, under normal circumstances, probably wouldn't have lived to tell the entire story.

David begins by telling how, as a ten year old boy, he lived through everything that led him from an occupied Holland to the West Indian tropics. Gradually the mature man steps forward who looks back on his past, and in the final chapters he sheds light on his rescuers, partly against the backdrop of what third parties published about them.

David Cohen would like to dedicate this book to his children and grandchildren.

He and the undersigned express our gratitude to Arie Lalleman, Steffi Cohen, Ron Veeninga, Uzi Hagai, Eli Katz, and Hans de Vries for their interest and critical reading of the manuscript.

Robert Lemm, Spring 2013.

Kfar-Saba, May 1999

My dearest Imri,

First of all I want to tell you how touched I am the way you sang your parsha. I am very proud that I have such a wonderful grandson, who is now grown up according to the Jewish tradition. I am very happy that this occasion gave us the possibility to be here all together, and that we could come over from Holland and the USA thanks to your loving parents and sisters. This is your special week, Imri. A few days ago you did your presentation at school about your roots, which was also very interesting. Maybe, Imri, it is thanks to the Rembrandt that we are all here now. Only God will know.

Love, Saba.

1. The Beginning

The Bar Mitzvah of my grandson was an event that deeply touched me. Our family had travelled from the Netherlands and the United States to Israel. It was very emotional to see how he talked about his roots in Holland at school, about the history of his grandfather and mother, uncles and aunts, about how they had survived the war thanks to a Rembrandt painting.

The story of my survival dates back to the second year of the occupation, in Dieren. Hearing about it again in Kfar-Saba in Israel made me relive my past, with my uncles Benjamin and Nathan, and the painting. It was a piece of Jewish history I was a part of, which I want to remain a part of. My grandson's Bar Mitzvah also made me think back to my own Bar Mitzvah that made me enter Jewish Life. I considered it to be a clear choice. Now I am standing here in Israel and think of the wars and the conflicts my children and grandchildren have to deal with. Again that choice! Remaining true to your identity and keep up the fight to openly carry it out.

My story began when we, as a family, silently got into the car. My parents, brother, my sister, and me. Somehow I felt that this wasn't an ordinary holiday trip to Zandvoort or Apeldoorn, to the playground. This time we would go somewhere far from home, a place we would probably never see again. My father sat in the front with my brother on his lap, next to the driver. I was sitting in the back, in between my mother and sister. Not a word was said, and questions were roaming around in my head. We had to say goodbye to my grandmother and everyone else who stayed behind, and to my dog; I hoped the family we had left him at would take good care of him. We didn't bring a lot of luggage; each of us brought only one suitcase filled with clothes, nothing more. Where were we going? My parents didn't know. All we knew was that uncle Bij had taken care of everything. However, we realized too well that things could go wrong. Five cars were driving towards an uncertain future.

Finally we arrived in Amsterdam, a place I had never been to before. We got off at Hotel Hiegentlich, in the Hoogstraat, where we would spend the night. My uncle did not allow us to go out on the street. One of my older cousins was so excited he wanted to take a look around in town, but my uncle forbid him to do so because it was extremely dangerous. We stayed at the hotel for two days, and early in the morning we took the tram to Central Station. It was the first time I saw Amsterdam in broad daylight.

When we arrived at the station we found out that my uncle from Switzerland and uncle Bij had arranged with the Germans that a train was waiting for us with two reserved compartments. Our journey that started there turned out to be a nightmare. The windows of our compartment were blinded, and only our uncle seemed to know where we were going. He was in close contact with the high members of the SS who occasionally strolled through the aisles. My parents and other relatives had tense looks on their faces.

Who knew, perhaps we were sent to one of those work camps; from the reports that reached the home front, we had understood that this was a worst case scenario. However, at that point we had no idea about the large massacres, but vague forebodings made us shiver.

The one thing in that pitch black train that comforted us was the courteous treatment of our uncle by the German officers. Were they playing a game with us, or could we conclude from their treatment that we were safe from a dark fate? They gave us food and something to drink without having to pay for it. It seemed like they were giving us a preferential treatment. Still, it never took away our fears. Where were we going?

After a day we arrived in Paris. From the Gare du Nord they drove us to the Gare d'Austerlitz, and soon we travelled further south, but no longer blinded. What I can still clearly remember are the big black leather polished boots and the heavy grey coats of the German SS. Their uniforms were threatening, but at the same time they also gave us a sense of being protected, and gradually we became more confident that we would end up well. The well-off Germans in the train, among whom no other than Aus der Fünten and Willy Lages, gradually made us feel at ease. Yet, one heavily speculated about what would happen to us.

And that is how we reached the Spanish border. Before the yellow badges were removed from our clothes we had to pose for a military photographer with Aus der Fünten and Lages. The picture was taken on 21 October 1942, the day we crossed into Spain at Hendaye.

2. Spain

The removal of the badges relieved our anxiety now that we no longer had to identify ourselves as Jews. From Irun we travelled to Bilbao by train, where we would remain for three weeks in a large hotel named Carlton which was located on a square. Leaving the hotel was not advisable, but we did sometimes go out for a walk. The thing I remember of those promenades were the heavily mutilated people begging on the side of the road. It caused a strong emotional reaction, since I had never seen something like that before. Afterwards I understood that it had been the result of the Spanish civil war, an episode I knew nothing of back then. Another thing I recall were the German officers strolling through the streets because it was a fascist country, under General Franco. To the dismay of my parents the German army was clearly present, even though I heard that Franco had not allowed Hitler to occupy Spain as a transit to North Africa.

Afterwards I read that Hitler met Franco at the Spanish border accompanied by Joachim von Ribbentrop, a literate man who knew Don Quixote. He supposedly told the Führer that he had always thought the Spaniards resembled Don Quixote, but the moment he saw Franco he discovered they were more like Sancho Panza.

In Bilbao we had to wait for where we would go next. One day we were all outside for a walk when suddenly we heard people shouting, and finally saw a group of women pointing at us. They came towards us and tried to make us understand that some of our family members weren't dressed appropriately, yet at the time we had no idea what they were saying. It was so threatening, all these women surrounding us that we fled to the nearest hotel. It turned out that one of my nieces was wearing trousers, which, in the eyes of the Spanish women, made her look like a man, something which was not tolerated.

During our stay uncle Bij often visited the Dutch consulate, where they arranged our paperwork. Each family required individual permission and had to report independently. From the certificates of vaccination we learned that we would not remain in Franco's country.

One considered bringing us to Portugal, but in the end this turned out to be too risky because we could still be arrested. We felt displaced and unsafe. Eventually we got word from London that we were allowed to travel to Jamaica.

3. The Voyage at Sea

And so we boarded the train to Vigo, a port in the North West of Spain where we had to stay until the 14th of November when the Marqués de Comillas raised its anchor. It turned out to be a large passenger ship with mostly Spaniards on deck who had come from Gibraltar where they had been waiting at refugee camps. Jews from all over Europe who had crossed the Pyrenees on their own joined us as well. On board we also saw non-Jewish Dutch citizens, who, like us, fell under the authority of the Dutch government in London.

Our journey was not without danger because of the German destroyers that carried torpedos. So, only the moment we left the territorial waters of Europe behind we felt relieved. At least we weren't heading towards one of those sinister camps. Nor would we have to drift to finally be denied and forced to return to Europe, with all the misery involved, as stories from other refugees had made clear.

On board we joined uncle Benjamin Katz and his wife Marianne, and their thirteen children-in-law, and grandchildren, as well as uncle Bram from Apeldoorn with his wife aunt Jans, and three children. Including me and my parents, my brother Jacques and my sister Vrouwtje, there were twenty-five of us. We considered ourselves to be refugees among the refugees, together with people from Belgium and other European countries. Most of them had experienced far worse than us.

I began to realize that we occupied a privileged position that went along with several conveniences. For instance, the boat had an upper deck and a lower deck that were strictly separated. As children we didn't really care for the rules and my nephew Eli and I would often go out and investigate. For hours we roamed the decks of the boat. We feasted our eyes on all these different people with different nationalities; Polish, Spaniards, French, from every corner of Europe. However, we did share the fact that we had all ended up on this vessel because of the war, looking for a safe haven.

My mother never came out of her cabin during the trip. As soon as we left the port she got seasick, which lasted until she set foot on shore again. Aunt Jans, though, felt a lot better and would join the captain during diners.

We also had a swimming pool on board, which is where I learned to swim.

4. Jamaica

Our voyage at sea lasted about three weeks. Eventually we got the news that the Dutch and British governments had agreed in allowing the five hundred passengers, among whom more than two hundred Dutch citizens, to disembark in the port of Kingston in Jamaica, an island I had never heard of before. I also had no idea where it was geographically located, but that there were no Germans in sight, and that we were far away from all the violence, eased our minds as we approached the unknown. After arriving in the capital buses drove us through the mountains to a place where, as it turned out, many refugees had already been housed. It was called the Gibraltar Camp. On site there were more than one hundred barracks surrounded by two and a half hundred acres of land with around it a fence. It wasn't far from Kingston. Between eight in the morning and ten at night we got permission to leave. Close to our new abode was the village of Papine which was located at the Gibraltar Road.

At the end of 1942 we had landed in Jamaica, and for the few hundred Dutch citizens who did travel to Jamaica on the Marqués de Comillas, the Gibraltar Camp III had been established. It was especially designed for the escapees on their way to the Dutch colonies in the Caribbean, such as the Antilles and Suriname. We would stay here for almost a year.

Once we got settled we had the opportunity to go on regular trips, however, a pass was required. On the island I went to a 'boarding school', but we never spend the night there since we weren't internal students. It happened to be a Roman Catholic institute where a uniform was mandatory. Inside and outside of the camp we lived according to British traditions. Me, and nine other boys my age used to take the bus to school every day. My younger brother stayed behind and went to kindergarten. In the afternoon the bus drove us back to camp.

One of our teachers was called father Knight, a priest wearing a robe. He paid special attention to us, as Jewish children at a catholic school. He knew that we were Jewish, and that we had been forced to flee because of the war. The managing board maintained links with the administration of the Gibraltar Camp, which made sure that the children would be educated. What I remember is that I didn't want to kneel. I was ten or eleven years old, had had Jewish lessons in Dieren, and as a Jewish kid you do not want to bend your knees as Catholics do. Fortunately they never forced us to do so, a gesture which I always considered to be a form of tolerance because they took account of us. It was especially considerate since boarding schools in general were usually strict, so I have good memories of the short period we stayed there. I found it quite remarkable; I learned to speak English there. I had a talent for languages, which it made easy for me to join the rest of my class, even though at first I was very tired because everything was so new.

Initially I felt distressed and found the life from home particularly difficult. Eli really supported me during those days. In the weekends we would meet up with others and visit a town close to Kingston. Here we would drink coffee at a hotel or restaurant, and visit the market in Papine, where I was enraptured by the range of colorful clothing, and women with large baskets on their heads. We saw a man selling chickens, and when he did he would snap the neck of the animal he had just sold. The temperament of the people fascinated me. However, above all music and film left a lasting impression. The first film I saw, in color, was called *Hello, Frisco, Hello 1943* with Alice Faye and John Payne. The leading song read *You'll never know* and it became the first English song I knew by heart. My whole being opened and everything I saw and heard made me extremely happy.

Holland was far away and forgotten. However, my parents did not feel the same. They did'nt stop worrying and not a day went by where they didn't think of home or the fate of the family members who had stayed behind.

I never really paid attention to most of their deliberations and the organization of life in the camp. I let myself go because of the tropical climate. You could say that spring entered my life. Who or what ensured this spring I never truly noticed. I went to school and enjoyed myself. To a certain extent my father let loose too. He behaved relaxed, felt freer, and was able to be himself. He occasionally sat down for a drink, and had friends with whom he played cards and spend quite a night with. It was his way of distracting himself. He had to leave his parents and two sisters and their families behind in the Netherlands.

I experienced the island feeling entranced while my parents struggled to adapt. They, and our uncles and aunts only talked about who and what they were missing. Nothing else interested them and they felt no peace. It didn't matter that they were safe and far away from the war because the others were suffering. What that suffering entailed was something we discovered later

The sounds of the war never reached the Caribbean. The island slept in the sun even though on several occasions men were called to London for military service, Dutch men who would work for the Irene Brigade that operated from the United Kingdom. The people who didn't have to leave passed the time by chatting, playing games, and statute labor.

After a year uncle Bij, his wife, and youngest son left for New York, where a store of the Katz art trade was situated. The family fell apart. Me, my parents, my brother and sister, as well as my uncle Bram and his family from Apeldoorn moved to Curaçao. We could have gone to Suriname, or even Cuba, but in Willemstad we were offered a real home, and moving to the United States turned out to be too expensive.

5. Curaçao

A British army plane flew us to the Dutch Antilles which were guarded by the Americans. For me flying was a new experience. I can still hear the engines roar and smell the indefinable aroma of the enclosed area we stayed in. All windows were blinded which made looking outside impossible. The only thing you felt was how the plane moved and rose with a deafening noise. Once in the air we began to relax as the noises diminished and became monotonous. However, as the speed and sound increased, the tension increased as well. Did the engines just stop? After take-off landing was particularly exciting, and calm returned only the moment we set foot on Aruban soil.

In Curaçao we heard that the Katz family from New York had ensured our stay here. This was at the end of 1943. In Willemstad we lived in a house by the sea, where our family, and my uncle and aunt's family remained until the end of the war. I remember that, in one of the rooms, a Rubens painting was placed that had been send by uncle Bij from New York. It was sold to a notary and the proceedings paid for our expenses on the island.

In the meantime the spring of my life continued without interruption. Not only did I go to a public Dutch school, the feeling of me being Jewish flourished. Curaçao knew one small prosperous community of mainly Sephardic Jews, with such names as Maduro, Capriles, Cardozo, De Casseres, and Fernandes.

These names were like music to my ears because they echoed the sound of an exotic past that, in my imagination, harmonized with the warm surroundings of the Caribbean paradise. Under the sun and the palms I felt the firm beat of my young heart. Here we were living in our own house, with even two women who made sure the rooms were clean, bought us food and supplies and cooked.

On Curaçao I had my Bar Mitzvah in 1945 in the beautiful Mikvé Israel Emanuel Synagogue of the Dutch Portuguese Israeli parish. The day and that place are forever etched in my memory as the happiest of my life. The document of the church council that was addressed to my father read:

> *We acknowledge the receiving of your letter on July 6, in which you inform us that your son David wishes to celebrate his ecclesiastical age of majority on Saturday July 21. We enable you to have the Bar Mitzvah in our Synagogue, and suggest you discuss the details with our rabbi. We want to thank you for the invitation to the reception, which we hope to make use of.*
>
> *With regards,*
> *On behalf of the church*
> *The council president*
> *Morris D. Cardozo*
> *Secretary,*
> *Josey Capriles*

My father had gone all out to make sure the day would be unforgettable and the Rabbi had prepared me for joining the parish. I can still hear the voice of the chazzan, and how my own voice was carried through the synagogue in Curaçao while reading the parasha. I never felt more confident, every word I sang, I sang with conviction; I had studied it well and I sensed that my singing confirmed my identity as a boy. Never before I had felt so supported by my parents. I received many gifts and a lot of people came out to see me, among whom the Capriles and the Maduros we had met in Willemstad.

The yellow badge we wore in the Netherlands also had something to do with it, because it confirmed that we were particular, it implied a distinction, something that made us different from the others. That is why I sang with so much conviction, with my uncle Bram as my example. He taught me to embrace that identity, and thanks to his teachings I became closely connected to him. My voice even moved all those who came out to see me that day. They made me the center of attention, I was one of the adults now. However, what that really meant I only began to realize after returning to the Netherlands. What I appreciated most in my father was, despite the fact that he no longer felt Jewish or did anything to affirm his beliefs, he did everything in his power to make sure that day would be the highlight of my life.

Yet, as exciting as life on Curaçao had been to me with its abundance of languages, cultures, and scents, my parents did not share my happiness as they nervously waited until they could go back to the, in the meantime, liberated Holland. What were they still doing here? Especially my father, who had fallen ill, was unhappy. Within our family he had little to say, as he depended on the money of his brother-in-law in New York. For the first time ever I learned something about his character, how he constantly racked his brains and felt inferior.

Since he was a non-stop smoker he suffered from a throat disease that would, later on in the Netherlands, be fatal. It did not matter that my mother tried to reason with him, or that she protected him from her brothers, he was inconsolable.

After the excitement around my Bar Mitzvah my parents were no longer mentally capable of paying attention to us. They had their own problems; things we didn't understand as children. Through a series of telegrams they tried to uncover what had happened to their family members in the Netherlands. For us their investigations passed unnoticed. Even my sister, who had turned eighteen and already worked at an office, couldn't share their concerns while being too involved with friends and their male companions. We were young, and our lives were just beginning.

6. Back in Holland

In November word came from Holland that we could go home. I would have loved to stay on Curaçao, however, my parents and my aunt and uncle wanted to leave as soon as possible. They didn't care about the island, they were tired of counting down the days, and they knew that uncle Bij had already returned to the Netherlands. After receiving the necessary paperwork from England we boarded the Stuyvesant, a cargo vessel that also transported passengers. We travelled via Trinidad Tobago and Suriname, and our journey lasted for six weeks. Halfway they loaded oranges and bananas onto the vessel.

To me, going home turned out to be a culture shock. I came from a sunny paradise and entered the grey, post-war, and damaged Netherlands. I felt miserable. Would I ever be able to get used to this petty place again? I had seen the world, and the thought of going back to school here disturbed me. My parents, on the other hand, tried to resume their lives as soon as possible, they had finally returned home.

We were properly taken care of when we set foot on Dutch soil, and the first night in November of 1945 we stayed with family in Amsterdam. The second day we travelled by car to Apeldoorn and Dieren. Back in Dieren we discovered that our house was no longer habitable because it had been confiscated by the Germans during the occupation. My parents decided to remodel and improve it, and in the meantime we stopped at friends of my parents who had emerged from been in hiding.

All the furniture that had disappeared was replaced by new pieces. Our belongings and antiques, which had partly been stored with friends in Arnhem returned. But our village looked so sad. The Netherlands made a somber and grey impression in comparison to the blue skies of our warm islands. The worst part was the barely suppressed astonishment with which the people from Dieren welcomed us back.

One had clearly not considered the fact that we would return and the way they received our family made my parents feel very ashamed. The neighbors and others they had grown up with and the place where we were born finally showed their true colors. They took us for wealthy inhabitants who had returned from a holiday, while the ones who stayed behind had to endure the occupying forces and the hunger winter.

Upon arriving in the Netherlands we were told that a brother of my mother and his family had returned from the camp. My father's sister had outlived the war at a hiding place. Another sister, his oldest, had been killed with both her parents.

The relationship between the only sister of my father's parents who had survived was extremely tense. She was a widow and had moved from hiding place to hiding place with her four children. One of my mother's sisters died during the journey back from Bergen-Belsen.

After exactly three years we were finally home again. Yet, no one greeted the people who had lived through the camps, or were willing to listen to their stories. I myself did not experience this indifference. For most of us the only thing that mattered was that… we were back and could manage. As a result I never really suffered because of the rejection.

The fact that nobody talked about the recent past also played a role. Who wanted to hear what had actually happened? You just had to make sure you put food on the table and that money was made. Reconstruction became the key word after the war. One never asked about the people who had disappeared, no one seemed to miss them and never inquired where they had gone. Only the ones who, like my family, missed relatives were concerned. My father had lost both his parents, in addition to his sister and her husband.

What always struck me was that we, as children, never expressed any form of sorrow. I never saw my parents grieving, or mourning the absence of my grandparents. They knew which camps they had been sent to and realized what had occurred to them. The first thing they uncovered, already when we were still on Curaçao, was where they had been taken. But after the war one was mostly distracted by the material aspect of it all, and by what was still there. In retrospect I found it very peculiar that we … My father must have been terribly worried, and I think this aggravated his illness, because he was incapable to mourn the losses, and my mother also didn't know how to deal with it either. Her only sister had disappeared, and here they were, they had survived the war… They must have felt terribly guilty. That old grandmother Eva Katz Franken who had been sent to Westerbork, and was able to repatriate with the help of my uncle in Switzerland, however, died before my parents came back; and all that in addition to my mother's youngest brother and his wife, both of whom uncle Nathan had tried to safe with a painting, but in vain. He knew they had been transported to Westerbork, but he could not prevent them from being moved to their death in Bergen-Belsen.

Our status in Dieren also caused suppressed jealousy. My uncle Bij's business, where my father had continued his work in November 1945, did do well, even though they had to rebuild everything, with antiques and furniture and such. In the years after the war the circulation of 'dirty money' was quite common, and old paintings were in demand. It was true that you needed cash, but in the fifties the business flourished. My uncle Nathan died in 1949 in France, his wife and children decided to stay in Switzerland.

7. School Time

Despite the fact that I never completed primary school on Curaçao I was accepted at secundary education. After a year they even allowed me to enter the HBS, the *Higher Civil School* in Amsterdam. I could speak proper English and with it I loved to show off. Nonetheless, it never helped me because I had a hard time fitting in. I felt completely estranged from Dutch reality. Besides, at home I suffered from my father's deteriorating health, who, in 1948, after his long-term illness passed away.

My uncle Bij paid for his care and treatment at a hospital in Groningen, including the weeks my mother spent in a hotel to be close to him. In 1949, after my father's death, my sister Vrouwtje got married and moved to the Dutch East Indies with her husband.

Initially there were no forms of transportation so I was forced to travel to Arnhem with an army truck. Of course many others had to process the changes too, but going back to school turned out to be really difficult. The other students had learned to live with the situation at hand and had evolved. They enjoyed the fact that cars were being used again and that they could go to school, that food stopped being scarce; the Marshall help soon followed. The entire population exulted in the haze of the liberation we had never experienced. At the HBS one did not speak of the war. In hindsight I even found it really strange that we were taught to speak German and learn the grammar. I still remember my German teacher, Mr. Bolk, who acted very strict. But, at least he was Dutch and not German. I never forgot about him; we had French and English class, which was great, but German… They also taught us about the history of the world, but we never discussed the 1940 - '45 period. The contemporary history we were told about ran until the outbreak of the war. Only when the Nuremberg trials started in 1948, the terrible truth began to surface. We were confronted with it when the television was introduced, when we saw the images. Before 1950 nobody talked about the war. Not that it had never happened, but attention was focused on the reconstructions which were the only thing that mattered.

At least the HBS turned out to be a relief after the terrible Mulo I went to in Dieren, where, for some reason I did not fit in. Thanks to the efforts made by the head of the HBS, Mr. Roorda, I was accepted. However, because I had to look after my mother I could not finish my degree. I wasn't able to prepare myself for my exams. Those days I also saw a nerve doctor, at the time I attended the fifth grade, the most difficult one. Studying became a nightmare, I struggled with myself, while worrying about my mother in the hospital.

The nerve doctor never really understood what was wrong with me, it had something to do with my sexuality, with my desire for friends. But I never talked about that, and the doctor never asked. He blamed everything on my sick mother and the fact that I was unable to keep up at school. He thought me a little too sensitive, I needed to loosen up.

He was a kind man, and I really appreciated that I could go see him, but he never truly tried to uncover what was going on inside of me. He could have discovered that there was something else wrong with me than a lack of glutamic acid. But the word sexuality did not exist at that time. He happened to be a very renowned nerve doctor, but in the fifties one simply did not discuss sexual maturity. At school I never talked about my treatment.

At school I joined a jazz band, the immediate result of my time in the Caribbean. At the same time the swing was introduced, the one I had already seen in the Caribbean. The glamour-like atmosphere attracted me, the rhythm of the music, the feeling of something new that the United States introduced to us with films. I saw all of them. It was my dream world. After having returned to Holland I met some people at the HBS who were also fascinated by it. After the war American music, the Jazz, became also fashionable in Europe, especially in the fifties. And against this backdrop I became part of a band, performed at gigs, and even won during a contest. Our band also performed in Dieren once at an exhibition of my uncle's business in 1952. Focusing on music proved to be my only relief.

8. Growing Up

I was longing for my childhood years in the tropics where happiness seemed to last forever. My plan even consisted of moving to the United States as soon as possible, since that was where I would fit in. Music and film were what made me want to leave.

Another form of escapism for me was tennis. In Dieren one of my friends' parents, the daughter of family Breuking of the Gazelle factory, made sure that we would play in the park behind our house. That is how I became a member of the tennis club at fourteen years of age, when I enlisted in a team that took part in competitions which enabled me to travel outside of Dieren, to Arnhem for instance.

Tennis and music really helped to entertain myself with, in the company of my friends. It made me forget all the difficulties. Nonetheless, sometimes it was hard to completely let go.

I keep remembering my father as a very introverted man. Whether he felt like the lesser person because of his marriage, or to what extent he felt troubled by it, I cannot say. I guess it was part of it, but he never really said so or complained about it.

I must confess though that I had little personal contact with him, which was also a consequence of the war. Possibly because, ever since we left Holland in 1942, we had always been on top of each other, first during our journey abroad, and then during the camp life in our barrack.

Besides, we had been forced to put up with the whole family most of the time and never only with our parents, always as a group of twenty-five. Only after the war, back at home, we were amongst ourselves again for the first time.

My father was a chain smoker, even despite of the fact that the doctor had told him to stop he simply continued. We lived in a house with a terrace and a staircase that led downstairs, and at the garden fence there was a large oak tree. Standing on that terrace I could see how he, while hiding behind that tree, before he walked to work, would secretly light a cigarette. My mother asked me to keep an eye on him. At home we talked about it because he coughed continuously. My mother hated it. Eventually they diagnosed him with throat cancer after which he had to be admitted to a hospital. At that time my mother still managed to be present while he was in surgery. Those days broke my heart because we were living on our own in that large house with only a maid to keep us company. In the meantime I had to go to school as I really wanted to finish the HBS.

After my father's death we were able to keep our house, thanks to uncle Bij. We had lost all contact with uncle Nathan in Switzerland; only his wife, my aunt, would return to the Netherlands.

At first I didn't have any trouble making my homework, but when my mother fell ill, concentrating became more and more difficult. She had someone who took care of her, and I never left her side. If I wasn't there my brother Jacques looked after her, but I couldn't make him do everything on his own because he was too young to do so. We had two maids, one of whom stayed during the weekends. My mother, therefore, always had company and someone to keep an eye on her. Several of my family members also frequently stopped by to pay her a visit, among whom a non-Jewish niece, in whose house my grandmother had lived during the war.

I would return on Sunday nights by train after I had spent the weekend at uncle Bram's in Apeldoorn. On my way back I did the homework I wasn't able to do in my room. That is why I always took my books with me, but I never really got to reading and working. My mother spoiled me, we were really close.

She was the first person I could express my feelings to. Living without me didn't enter her mind, she depended on me. I accompanied her through her entire illness, even when she was hospitalized in Velp. After school I would travel, before going home, from Arnhem to Velp, until they admitted her. She had to undergo surgery because of a bowel disease, and for years her problems would continue. I had to be careful to move on with my own life, yet my mother's long illness took a hold of me.

Deep down I felt remorse. Did I pay enough attention to her? At the time I acted as I pleased because it was in my nature. But it always made me feel guilty. Am I really allowed to do my own things? I asked myself. Although my mother wanted me to have everything I desired, in hindsight she did blame me. The same attitude I later found in Steffi. She always seemed to approve of what I wished to do – just do it, go -, but after coming home I understood she wasn't happy about it. My mother acted the same way; she played with my sense of responsibility but I kept doing what I wanted. I wouldn't let anyone take away my only outing.

My nephew Eli and I remained close friends after the war, since we were peers and brought up together. Apeldoorn proved to be my only way to relax as it enabled me to escape Dieren. It was a different world with dancing and music. On Saturday night Eli and I would go out and visit clubs with our friends. On Sunday nights I returned home. My mother didn't like it if I stayed out for long. At the time I was fourteen or fifteen years old. Uncle Bram, my substitute father, would visit his brothers at the business on Saturday, and he would take me with him as he returned home. It was a fixed pattern, and if homework would prevent me from going to Apeldoorn I would be really upset.

Those years were troublesome and that is why uncle Bram became very important to me; he was the role model I needed during that period. I craved for attention and guidance. He was religious in his own way and wore a cap. On Friday nights, when I visited him, he would bless us with a prayer after diner.

My sister had moved to Amsterdam in 1946 where she lived with an aunt and took some classes. She felt like she had to get away from Dieren. In Amsterdam she met my brother-in-law, and some time later they left for the Dutch East Indies, to return in 1950, shortly after my father's death. At first she came to us to help me take care of our mother, but in the end she permanently settled in Amsterdam.

Despite the fact that I never finished my degree I soon followed them to Amsterdam when I was twenty years old. With the help of a befriended doctor I made sure that I never had to serve in the army. An acquaintance enabled me to become an intern at a garment factory in Haarlem, and subsequently I found a job in a showroom in Amsterdam. Here I worked until I met Steffi. We never really hit it off at first, but one of our bosses brought us together, and eventually set us up.

9. Marriage

Because my marriage coincided with the death of my mother and the illness of my father-in-law, grief prevailed over joy in the liberal Jewish synagogue of rabbi Jaap Soetendorp at the Lairessestraat in Amsterdam. I then counted twenty-five years. My brother Jacques, who lived above our store in the Kinkerstraat, and I were very close. In my masculine world he helped and supported me, and Steffi also liked him very much.

From now on a new responsibility rose so quickly that I didn't get the time to feel like myself again. Since my mother's death I had to leave the house and moved in with my parents-in-law at the Michelanglostraat. My father-in-law who considered me to be the son he never had, gave me a leading function in his women's clothing store which meant I should keep up myself in between him and the staff. Because of his disease he was often absent, but if he would unexpectedly show up I could behave very nervously. He was a tyrannical Prussian who did not tolerate criticism, and the staff bowed down to him. It always surprised me that he had accepted me in spite of my introvert character and my lack of experience. I wasn't exactly the type in which he would see his desired likeness. However, I must have been a diamond in the rough because he treated me with more respect than anyone else. He was twenty years older than his wife, and could have been Steffi's grandfather. Before he escaped

Germany in 1933 he had controlled his parents' department stores.

How he and his family survived the war in Amsterdam I will disclose in the next chapter.

My father-in-law's business came into our hands after his death. In the second year of my marriage Sylvia was born, two years later Lilian followed, and three years later came Dennis. My daughters moved abroad; the oldest to Israel, the second to Australia. Apparently they felt Holland wasn't their home either. It was something applicable to Steffi and me as well. Yet, we were no longer in a position to make that change.

My children had close ties to Haboniem, a Jewish youth association, and we were all members of the liberal Jewish community. So my children came into contact with peers whose parents had experienced terrible things. Yet in this ambience one did not talk much about the past. Perhaps later my children learned about some of it from their friends in Israel. We encouraged them to go there, to Aliyah. Especially my oldest daughter; not my second one who moved to Australia. Lilian had no desire to learn anything about the war, neither about Zionism. My son, who also had been a member of Haboniem, would only start discussing recent history much later, in 1996, as a result of the video conferences that dealt with survival stories, in the framework of the Holocaust Project by Steven Spielberg.

We could have emigrated to Israel ourselves, but then we should have gone right away after 1945. During the Korean War several of our family members even considered emigrating to the United States. Yet, once again having to move to someplace new was the last thing my parents thought about. They were too relieved to be home at last.

I buried myself in my daily work. I concentrated on my staff and my family which enabled me to engage in a civil life that from A to Z followed the same rituals; my children's school life, the holidays at Noordwijk aan Zee, the tennis club. The only thing I permitted myself was the yearly weekend to the North Sea Jazz Festival, as a consequence of my years at the HBS in Arnhem and the everlasting love for jazz that our band had given me. The rest of our free time we spent on taking care of my mother-in-law, which we did for a very long time because she would only die when she was ninety-six in 1998. Her proximity deeply affected the course of our life.

But was this really all to be expected? Everything seemed to occur in patterns that were almost impossible to break, even though I knew I was responsible for it myself. My marriage, my work, my children, my hobbies… Was that it? When I looked around and saw the others, who had a life similar to mine, when I met some of my family members, who, like us, kept quiet in terms of their past, I never felt like I had any right to complain. We had survived the war. What was left to be said? Who cared about my story? How on earth had I been able to reach any returnee from one of the camps with my case? I had been lucky! And there were so many other survivors too who hid their past, the ones who had gone into hiding, for instance.

But it had taken a hold of me. There was something unsatisfactory about the circumstances that I found myself in. Only the years on Jamaica and Curaçao meant something I thought had been worth living for. But those years lay far behind me, belonging to a previous life I no longer had ties to.

My father had once decided to work for his brothers-in-law, who were tradesmen, and now I also found myself in the business life thanks to my wife. I never really thought about that parallel. I never wanted to think about it, because I always had the feeling that we, my father and I, came from a background that was worthwhile as well. Although we came from a poorer branch, and depended on the Katz family - and even though everything that had happened as a consequence of the war was financed by the Katz-brothers, I always felt a part of the whole family, and had never been aware of the fact that I owed them something. That because of Steffi something similar had happened to me I consider to be mere coincidence.

10. Steffi

Hotel Silve. We thought it pretty normal that I had been there as well, which is why we never discussed it. Our evacuation to Beekbergen, to Hotel Silve... it happened to be the same place Steffi was staying at, at the time. But when it came up years later, we decided that circumstance to be a coincidence. Why had she been there of all places, from Amsterdam, with her parents? I remember that in those May days the weather was lovely. She had spent quite some time there. Her father feared that the city would be bombed, and therefore he had taken refuge with his family at the Silve. Afterwards we learned that Rotterdam had been the target for the German bombs. We, on the other hand, had chosen to leave Dieren in order to be as far away as possible from Arnhem since that was where the Germans had invaded our country.

Steffi and I never ran into each other in the hotel, we didn't know either of us existed. Only years later, after our engagement I heard that she was taken there by her parents. She also had her own war episode. She and her family were turned into Aryan's, and had been placed on the Calmeyer list - for those declared non-Jews, or only partly Jewish - with her parents. At the start of the occupation everyone had to fill out forms which determined if you were Jewish or not. If you had four, three, or two Jewish grandparents, and if you were registered at an Israeli church community, you were, in the eyes of the Germans, Jewish. How she received the Aryan declaration is a remarkable story. She talked about it in the Shoah program, Steven Spielberg's video project which was made between 1995 and 1998. Here she, as precisely as possible, discusses what happened. A while ago I found a piece in the Dutch newspaper *Het Parool*, where they portrayed Mr. Calmeyer as a hero, someone who rescued Jews, even though that wasn't the entire truth. Later on one decided how to characterize this man, just like they did with Schindler and Weinreb. They even honored him via Yad Vashem. On Calmeyer's list Steffi was placed, and she owes her life to it.

Her story, in her own words, goes as follows: I was born on 14 March 1934. My parents came from Germany and had moved to the Netherlands in 1933, the year in which Hitler succeeded Hindenburg. They had some money which enabled them to enter the country. During their escape my mother became pregnant. My father, Hugo Weinbaum, was nineteen years older than my mother, and I often considered him more to be my grandfather. He came from an East Prussian workers family and had dictatorial tendencies. My mother came from a well to do background. Her family owned a chain of department stores in Germany. Because of their marriage my father was given the control of the Schönbeck department store in Nordhausen. My mother, Hildegard Goldstein, had married him in 1925 in the synagogue of Eisleben.

I was the child my parents had waited a long time for. Initially we lived at the Parnassusweg in Amsterdam, after which we moved to the Kinkerstraat, where they took over a clothing store. My parents had to leave Nordhausen in a rush because anti-Semitism was on the rise there. Later on my dad told me that they had poisoned his dog, and that they had beaten him at the train station before they boarded. For quite some time people decided to no longer buy their clothes in a Jewish store. My father's family, who was poor, stayed behind. He had seven brothers and seven sisters, who all died in the camps. My mother was one of four girls, two of whom emigrated to the United States, and one to Australia.

My parents had chosen the Netherlands because it had remained neutral during the First World War, something they thought would happen again during another war. Although my father came from a religious family, he did nothing to affirm his faith in Amsterdam. My mother came from a liberal family. As a child my parents sent me to the Montessori school. This school was located close to my grandparent's house, who had moved to the Parnassusweg in 1939 as well.

In the meantime we had settled in a large dwelling above our shop in the Kinkerstraat. My father took me to school every single day, or I took a taxi, which was, at the time, still relatively cheap. At home we spoke German. My dad worried about his relatives in Germany, whom he would never hear from or see again. The Dutch Jews avoided us; after all, they were already struggling to keep themselves going amongst the Dutch population, that did not like any newcomers. Even though we knew that there were a number of German Jews living close by, they never contacted us. As a young girl of six – Holland had been occupied for a year already – I did not feel any of the tensions.

Only at our home I often heard my parents complain, scream, and argue. Our being Jewish remained outside our scope, except for the fact that we didn't eat pork.

In 1942 my father had to report to an office at the Euterpestraat, which would later on become the Gerrit van der Veenstraat, to collect our yellow badges. Here he laughed at the serving German bureaucrats, while emphasizing he was a Prussian: 'Hier lachen Sie nicht, hier lachen wir,' (You do not get to laugh here, we do) they told him. Feeling shocked he returned home with three sets of badges. I was proud of my star, however, it did mean I had to go to a Jewish school, because I could no longer play with other children. That is how I transferred to the Jewish Montessori School at the skyscraper at the Merwede Square. The type of children that joined me in class differed from what I was used to. Here they behaved roughly, they played with knives, and sometimes children even disappeared, and I never understood why or where they had gone. At home I heard my parents talk about leaving or going into hiding. During the final days of 1941 a Verwalter (an administrator) visited us who would take over my father's business. We moved to the Michelangelostraat. However, my father still visited his store at the Kinkerstraat, because the Verwalter, Herr Friedrich, was a nice man, too nice in the eyes of his superiors. His wife had once been a servant for a Jewish family, and he kept good memories of those days. The Germans found this extremely offensive, and did not trust him. As a result they brought in another Dutch administrator who could keep an eye on him.

My father did not want to go into hiding. In the store a window dresser had told him he knew a place where they could flee, in the middle of the woods, in a castle. We had already packed our bags, but at the last minute my dad hesitated. It sounded too good to be true, and the plan was abandoned. Later on he became even more suspicious, it had to be a trap. The window dresser turned out to be related to the pro German NSB. The letter he wrote to god knows whom, about our refusal to go, thankfully never led to our deportation.

Nonetheless, our life remained extremely precarious. It was 1941, and the raids hadn't started yet. But what didn't happen today, could still happen tomorrow.

Fate came in the form of a German officer. One day he walked into our store when my father was standing behind the counter. It turned out that this man had a Dutch girlfriend, someone named Koosje Hanneman. He could tell from my father's accent that he came from East Prussia.

They engaged in a friendly conversation. When asked how business was going my father said: Not well… Why not? …Because I am a Jew... Sie sind keine Jude (You aren't a Jew), the officer answered, I will prove it to you! The officer, Doctor Wander, worked for Herr Calmeyer, who in turn was an official of the occupying forces, and the one in the Netherlands who could determine who he wanted to save. He altered the information of one's grandparents, reduced them from three to two, and gave you a couple of Christian grandparents in return. Of course you couldn't be associated with a Jewish Ecclesiastical community. Fortunately my parents weren't registered at one, since they, as stated before, did nothing to reaffirm their faith in the Netherlands. Calmeyer worked in The Hague, and one of his subordinates was Doctor Weinhart, the racial expert. He happened to be the one who would label us: he would measure us to determine if we were Jewish or not.

One day Herr Wander and his lover Koosje visited us at the Kinkerstraat. Sie sind keine Jude (You are not a Jew), he told my father once again. He considered it to be a joke from a nice man.

However, Wander gave him a card with Koosje's address, at the Rivierenbuurt. They would take care of the rest. My father visited her place twice and during the conversations it became evident that an Aryan declaration was expensive, very expensive, because we needed five of them. For my grandparents, my parents and me. It is possible that Koosje had financial interests in the transaction given the fact that she was addicted to morphine.

Via Wander my parents came into contact with a chemist who fabricated love letters on old paper from which it had to be clear that my father had been conceived by a non-Jewish lover of his mother. Similarly my mother was supposed to have one Jewish parent.

When the documents were ready we travelled to The Hague where someone had arranged for us to meet Mr. Calmeyer.

I still remember the five of us, wearing our yellow badges, travelling from Amsterdam to The Hague by train. In the office we heard that photographs were added to the love letters emphasizing we had other great-grandparents than we initially thought. When the papers were ready we had to visit The Hague once again in order to receive our Aryan declaration for 750 guilders per person. During our second visit we met lady Appelman, Doctor Weinhart's secretary, who had been informed by Wander that we were coming, and who played with the doctor's greed. But even then matters could not be settled yet. We had to wait for months before the proper documents came. Months filled with doubts. Could we trust Wander and Weinhart?

Eventually the time had come. Again we travelled to The Hague where we were given the papers that would save our lives. When we entered the room my mother almost fainted, because she recognized Doctor Weinhart as the teacher of her school in Germany. He had taught her sister. He was a science teacher and knew they were Jewish, but lady Appelman nodded encouragingly. When Weinhart recognized my mother as the sister of the woman he had considered to be a mathematical genius he called out: Ich habe immer gewusst dass Liesbetchen keine Judin ist; kein Jude ist ein Genie (I have always known that she isn't a Jew, after all no Jew could be considered to be a genius). And there we were, wearing our yellow badges. Yet we got our documents, which stated that we had two Christian great-grandparents, and two Jewish great-grandparents. Doctor Weinhart had understood perfectly. We returned home and no longer had to wear our stars because from that moment on we were Aryan. Our store no longer needed a Verwalter, because my father could run his own store again. And I no longer had to go to a Jewish school.

Meanwhile time had gone by and we found ourselves at the end of 1943. I went to the Dalton School in the Jan van Eyckstraat, where nobody thought me to be Jewish. My mother warned me that I couldn't talk to anyone about it. Once, when I was in the hospital I accidentally spilled our secret, but fortunately it didn't have any consequences.

My parents kept taking very good care of me. However, when there were raids we did hide in the basement. One time the Germans entered our house, and I remember that they focused on a photograph on the wall of my grandmother who, they believed, resembled Queen Wilhelmina.

Doctor Wander's life unfortunately ended tragically. He was an officer, but at the end of 1943 he deserted because he refused to serve at the eastern front. He didn't believe in the Nazi regime and had gone into hiding at Koosje's house. During the final days of 1944 they entered her house, and when he tried to escape via the staircase they killed him. We owe him our lives. After the war he was given a posthumous award in Israel, of Yad Vashem. They never told me that the Germans had killed Doctor Wander.

The final years of the war passed without problems. My father went to work every day, like every other Dutch citizen. The customers, who initially had known we were Jews, seemed to have forgotten this fact. After the liberation we were often critiqued for our attitude, especially from the communist side. Because in their eyes we were simply German, even though we had been stateless since 1933. When we raised our flag in 1945, they took it down. We weren't Dutch citizens, and would therefore be free from paying taxes. When I was thirteen, in 1945, I succeeded in acquiring the Dutch nationality via an exam. In

1948 our entire family acquired the Dutch nationality. Despite all the tragedies my parents still felt more German than Dutch, even though they had to escape.

The terrible truth of 1940 - '45 we gradually became aware of after the war. We read the Dutch newspapers *Het Parool* and *Het Vrije Volk*, and we listened to the radio. We never heard from our relatives. On the other hand, we did begin to realize that almost all the German Jews had been deported out of Amsterdam.

First I went to the Geert Groteschool, after which I changed to a domestic school. In 1952 I travelled abroad for the first time to London, where I worked as an *au pair* for a noble family. When I came back my father fell ill. With my mother I visited Switzerland.

We never spoke about the war.

I worked as a salesperson and bookkeeper at my father's store. For relaxation I contacted other Jews, until I ran into my husband. Through one of the bosses at the store I met David Cohen. They felt he needed a wife, and that I needed a husband. I actually preferred his younger brother Jacques, but when I came back from England David gave me a call. My mother had her doubts. After we had been introduced twice I didn't hear from him for quite some time, and she wondered if he was the right one for me to marry. But in the end they only thought one thing to be essential: that I married a Jewish man. It happened in 1958, in the liberal synagogue.

11. Why us?

The fact that we had survived, that we belonged to the small group of Jews who had emerged from the massacre of 1940 -'45, bound my fate to that of my wives', who, in a different way, had been just as fortunate as I was. Our pasts were intertwined, other than those of my sister and her husband – who had become traumatized in an Indian camp, after which she had to endure his nightly screams. However, Steffi and I were evenly matched; yet, what we shared we never discussed with others openly. Anyone who would have experienced the camps, would be uninterested in our story; and our fellow citizens, who had remained behind shouldn't feel like we were different from them. That said in hindsight, because at the time their indifference really disappointed us. We intuitively knew that they didn't want to hear about our years during the war; and if it came up, we kept the surface intact. The fact that, in a short amount of time, we had lost my grandparents, my aunts, my mother's sister, and her family members, we rather kept to ourselves. We realized, as previously stated, that it was terrible enough not to have been able to mourn them properly after the war. After all, didn't life simply go on? We behaved like everyone else, we pushed our past aside. We even barely talked to our children about it. We never gave them the opportunity to ask questions, and they never asked. As they got older, and became curious by what they had heard about it at school, it was too late. There was nothing, there wasn't a story. Should I have told them how exceptional I thought it was that I got married, had children, and could take care of others?

But should children be left behind not knowing? The shame and the guilt, the gratitude and a feeling of liberation formed an inextricable web. Why us?

Many survivors asked themselves that very question. But how did it work for us? The dead could ask us that question. Whatever the answer might be, it would never be like before.

We were scarred for life, each of us in our own way.

When I look back, my childhood years appear to be an unattainable domain. Life happened in a time that seems incomprehensible these days. We inhabited a large villa in Dieren on the banks of the river IJssel. My father worked in my uncle's business, who traded in antiques and specialized in the old masters. He came from an environment of small tradesmen; his grandfather had been a merchant in Doesburg. Because of his marriage he was included in the established circle of my mother's family. Her brothers belonged to the residents of Dieren.

Nothing would happen in town without my uncles being involved in one way or the other. Being a part of the wealthy section of society suited me – even though I was standing on the sideline as a child. Only later I realized, to the dismay of some, that within our family not everyone was held with the same high regard.

As inaccessible and introverted as my father had been, that is how open and optimistic my mother was. How my father dealt with it, had always been hidden. And similar to how he had ended up in the business life because of his wife that is how I, also because of my wife, ended up in a comparable situation.

12. Jewish Life in Dieren

Our presence in Gelderland, I read in Hans Kooger's book, dates back to the end of the eighteenth century. During the French occupation the discriminatory measures against the Jews were lifted, and after the proclamation of the kingdom, communities arose that made room for cemeteries and synagogues. Only five Jews still lived in Dieren around 1810, whereas more than three hundred could be counted in Nijmegen. These had their own synagogue, where the largest part of the Jews from Gelderland were registered. The ones who settled in this province during the first half of the nineteenth century, were mainly merchants, peddlers, and butchers. They had crossed the eastern border and came from Germany, and even from Poland and Russia. In those days Yiddish was the lingua franca. Halfway through the nineteenth century the number of inhabitants of Dieren grew rapidly to one and a half thousand; and from 1868 on, when the railway tracks between Arnhem and Zutphen appeared, the town developed into a small city. In 1878 a number of leading Jews turned to the mayor with the request to exercise their religion in an old school building. Four years later the community of Dieren was officially recognized by the standing committee of the Dutch Israelite Society. A new synagogue arose and the initiation feast turned into a ball in a room of Hotel De Kroon. Before the war the Jewish community amounted to approximately sixty members. Shortly after the outbreak of the war the Thora scrolls were hidden, and the building had been so badly damaged during the occupation that it could be considered a miracle it was still standing when the German forces left town. In 1973, the year of the restauration, the number of Jews could be counted on one hand. The few who did return in 1945 all left Dieren soon after. And all that remains of Jewish life there, is a small cemetery on the other side of the railway tracks, at the edge of a forest where a new residential area is built. That cemetery, a clear rectangle surrounded by barbed wire and a hedge is not even filled for more than 25%. The most recent stones belong to my parents, Casper Isaac Cohen and Mina Katz, in addition to those of my sister and her husband.

Hitler made me and my family Jews. My parents had said their goodbyes to the orthodox way of living they had grown up with the moment they got married, as most did during the pre-war years. People no longer seemed to visit the synagogue which made one believe that the absentees were no longer even devout at all. No more than two or three children showed up during the religious classes. I, like my five year old sister, went to a public school and during the Shabbat we continued cycling. The only restriction was that we couldn't cycle in front of my grandmother's house, who regretted our non-religious upbringing. Everything that reminded me of the chosen people converged in Apeldoorn. All the Shabbat meant to us consisted of paying extra attention to dinner and the distribution of candy.

My mother, Mina Cohen Katz, originated from a large family who, as previously mentioned, traded in old art. Her father, David Katz, my grandfather, was born in Doesburg in 1858. Early on he developed a passion for farmer's antiques. He married Eva Franken, with whom he had eight children, among who Benjamin and Nathan. In 1900 he opened a small store in Dieren, and thirty years later Benjamin and Nathan expanded that little store into Kunsthandel Katz, in the Spoorstraat 33-37, where they specialized in paintings, in particular those of seventeenth and eighteenth century masters. Occasionally they would organize an exhibition on Sundays in a showroom where they displayed work from, among others, Rembrandt, Frans Hals, Van Goyen, Rubens, Van Ostade, and many other Dutch and foreign masters. Regularly, people from towns outside of Dieren would stop by to admire the paintings.

The Katz brothers would also occasionally allow others to borrow their paintings for exhibitions elsewhere. In the summer of 1936, for instance, they sent fifty-seven masterpieces to Nijmegen, where, at the Belvoir mansion at the Lodewijk square, an exposition had been organized by the Waalbrug committee. Among the pieces were works painted by Joos van Cleve, Albert Bouts, El Greco, Rembrandt and Rubens, Jan Steen, Gerard Terborch, Ruysdael, Avercamp, Breughel, Nicolaas Maes, Murillo, Paulus Potter, and Jan van Scorel. All the works of art came with the documentation of their origin. The Rijksmuseum in Amsterdam succeeded in borrowing twenty pieces during the same period.

In the course of the summer of 1938 approximately one hundred paintings were lent to the salon Arti et Amicitiae in Amsterdam, among which paintings by Rembrandt, Anthony van Dyck, Ruysdael, Gerard

Dou, Albert Cuyp, Gabriel Metsu, Aert van der Neer, and Adriaen van Ostade. In the catalogue one could see the pictures of the works, introduced with a foreword written by the Firma D. Katz, which sounded as followed: 'By exhibiting these works, chosen from the ever expanding collection, we (the Firma Katz) hope to contribute something to the growing appreciation and interest for old paintings in wider circles. We constantly keep in mind to purchase only the best that can be found in this area at home and abroad. The revenues of the exhibition are entirely reserved for the Fund of Special Necessities in Amsterdam.' The Firma D. Katz was prominently present in Dieren and even got a royal distinction. Soon the brothers became famous abroad and chain stores were established in Basel and in New York, and on 1 May, 1940 they opened a store in The Hague.

The early thirties were not exactly the right time for business, however as the war approached the trade, specifically with the eastern neighbors, began to flourish. The Germans turned out to be avid collectors and soon the value of the paintings increased.

During the war the desire for art increased even more, something the Firma Katz profited from. The interest came in particular from the art trader Alois Miedl, and Hans Posse, director of the Gemäldegalerie in Dresden, who were both closely related to the Nazi top. Of the two Miedl was the most independent, and known to be rather unreliable. He would soon, as Verwalter, take over the business of the famous Amsterdam art dealer Jacques Goudstikker, which put pressure on my uncles.

Shortly after the capitulation Dr. Posse had moved to the Netherlands. This doctor happened to be the executive who put together the collection for the Führermuseum in Linz, and he never hesitated to approach Jewish art dealers. Those contacts would soon become of vital importance to our family, because my uncles quickly realized what could happen to the Jews. And that is why and how they used their art to save their lives.

The German's thirst for paintings seemed unquenchable, and mainly seemed to focus on the celebrated masters, the elevation of the human being to a higher plan. From everywhere they brought in exemplary scenes to illustrate their noble endeavor. As a result, art dealers could count on their eagerness. Before and during the war Miedl played a dubious role in these matters. The Jewish companies were abolished or changed into Aryan companies, something that also happed to Goudstikker's store. The 'Paintings and Antiques trade' of my uncles was simply abolished.

However, for a short period, the Katz Brothers, in terms of their relationships at home and abroad, remained the individuals to go to when it came to the acquisition of the old masters. That fact turned out to be the starting point for negotiations that, eventually, wouldn't be about money, but about human lives.

In September my uncle Nathan Katz told Dr. Posse that he could mediate the purchase of a major assortment in Switzerland. It concerned the collection of Otto Lanz which was managed by his widow. Posse had been given some million francs to enrich the museum of the Führer with masterpieces. And Otto Lanz' widow would only negotiate with my uncle. In exchange for mediation Nathan Katz would receive an exit visa for himself, his wife, and four children.

Some two or three months later they left. Once in Switzerland my uncle tried to acquire works for German clients, something which, after the war, was questioned by several. Nonetheless, they forget to take into account that Nathan Katz was merely accepted in Basel by the Swiss government because he donated paintings, and above all, one should not forget that he behaved very generously when it came to financial aid for fugitives. I will discuss the details and judgments later.

13. Reviving the Start of the Occupation

When I, as a small boy of eight, heard the roar of the airplane engines on that unfortunate tenth of May 1940, the babbling river of my life accelerated rapidly. We had just moved, because that same day we decided to flee with the entire family and take refuge in Beekbergen where we remained for five days at a hotel with a garden that resembled a castle called Silve. Why we had to do so nobody told us. Later on we heard that soldiers were fighting at the Grebbeberg, and that it was advisable to stay as far away from the battlefront as possible. We had to leave everything, but our clothes behind. The only thing that made me sad was the fact that I couldn't bring my dog. Other than that I thought it quite an exciting adventure.

Hotel Silve proved to be a haven for many from all over. Among them, accompanied by her parents, but unnoticed by me, the girl I would marry after the war.

Five days went by, and following the capitulation the police gave us permission to go home. The evacuation had ended, but on the streets we saw German soldiers. Gradually we began to realize that our country had been taken, something which made especially my parents very restless. They read the newspapers and knew what had happened across the border, but they never said a word about it to us because we were still too young to understand the severity of the events. I went back to school and played with my friends.

In January 1941 the reporting obligation for Jews was established. Not long after my uncle Nathan got his exit visa, so he left for Switzerland with his family. In this we saw an ominous foreboding. His wife, my aunt, had said that we all had to take care of ourselves, and God of all of us, something the family would resent her for, for quite some time. For them it was easy to talk like that, with their foreign relations. To reassure us uncle Bij promised then that he would take care of all of us. How he was able to stick to his promise is the key to this story.

Over the course of February 1942 I also began to feel that something had changed. My parents knew people from the NSB who, until then had kept quiet, but who now openly expressed their German sympathy. How to act around them? My sister was the first to notice the anti-Semitism. At the time they had left me in my daily routine, though this also changed when I was no longer allowed to assist to classes. We had to go to a separate school for Jewish children. Since there were only a few of us, it meant the end of my learning days. Fortunately one of our teachers who happened to live next door, offered to give private lessons to me and my brother. But my friends Wim and Herman started to treat me differently; and their parents preferred that they would not visit our home anymore. I also discovered that we could no longer move around as we pleased. For instance, the yellow badge prohibited me from going to my favorite playground in Apeldoorn, the Julianatoren, which I would often visit on weekends. With the exception of my brother, who at the time was too young to wear a star, we were marked.

Since, for the first time in my life, I was no longer permitted to go to school, I got a strong sense of my exceptional position. It was something I was already aware of, even as a child. And it gave me a feeling of being different, being particular. The negative side of that discrimination, which is basically what it was, did not come through to me. As a child I simply walked around with a star, so everyone could see I was Jewish. It even gave me a sense of self-worth because they still had to accept me. What it actually meant never got to me, so I developed mixed feelings about all of it. I never grieved over it. Yet, for my parents it was obviously quite different whereas they constantly worried about things to come.

Precisely during that year the threat came really close. The fear my parents felt finally took a hold of us as well, because there had been raids in Brummen, and stories circulated about Jews doing forced labor in the village of Ellecom. We were living not far from there in Dieren, so the first thing we thought was: when will it be our turn? Nevertheless, as a child you are not really confronted with it, you couldn't ask questions about it. You just kept on playing with other children on the street. The period between February and November passed too swiftly for me to really understand the circumstances and the threat. Life accelerated in a phantasmagorical way.

14. Preparations for our Departure

Uncle Bij had remained in Holland with the rest of the family. Getting out was becoming more difficult as the days went by. Over the course of 1942 the threat did only increase, and everywhere raids took place in order to deport Jews. In Dieren the danger had come so close that we slept at the attic of our neighbor's house for a couple of days. Fortunately the Germans never came for us, but the fear my parents felt was palpable. Our name and fame no longer guaranteed us a free pass, something the Katz family acutely realized.

At night, long after we had gone to bed, they would discuss all of it. The Katz family, who, in terms of Jewish inhabitants, with the Levie's and Bachrach's determined life in our town, had managed to keep in touch with foreign art dealers and collectors due to their work as experts and with their stores. Whenever I would walk through the Spoorstraat, alongside the large shop which had 'Paintings Antiques' written on the wall, I proudly told my friends where my father worked. The two enormous shop windows displayed a lot of paintings, and in the back, in the warehouse, there were many more placed in between the furniture and porcelain.

By way of the museum director and art agent Hans Posse, my uncle had uncovered that the German Reichsminister Hermann Goering wanted to buy a painting for the Führer. It happened to be a portrait of a man located in Switzerland. Immediately uncle Bij saw the opportunity for not only himself, but the entire family, to leave the country. And that is how he and uncle Nathan began to take action that would lead to our joint departure.

In a large villa close to Basel uncle Nathan had been able to continue his business. The fact that he and his wife were frequently included in several German circles explains how uncle Bij succeeded in removing us from Holland. Whereas uncle Bij might direct our exodus from beginning to end, uncle Nathan negotiated with the Nazis in Switzerland. He couldn't have done so had he lived in the Netherlands.

Right from the beginning Nathan Katz must have foreseen the threat hanging over our heads, but how he proceeded was something beyond my knowledge. The largest part of our family cherished the thought that things wouldn't come this far. My mother's youngest brother, for example, could have joined us with his wife, in addition to a child from Austria who was living in a house with my aunt, a Jewish girl whose parents had been deported. But her brother refused to go. He believed that the Katz name would protect him, and that the Nazis would leave him and the others alone. However, at the last moment they were arrested and deported to Bergen-Belsen; with my mother's older sister who had also decided not to leave the country, and who had just gotten married for the second time with the brother-in-law of my youngest uncle.

So my uncle Bij played an essential role in the transaction of the painting that saved us. He and uncle Nathan made sure it arrived exactly where the Germans wanted to have it. The only danger was that the German authorities in Holland could put a stop to the plan. In particular Willy Lages, the *SS Sturmbannführer*, and indeed *Generalkommisar für das Sicherheitswesen* Hans Rauter, the highest police chief, and one of the main officials in Holland, objected. But in the end our departure was enforced by the high entourage that surrounded Goering.

Which painting actually saved us had been unclear for quite some time; but now one repeatedly writes about it. Years ago I read several articles in the press about the Goudstikker affair. At the time I was involved in a documentary as a consequence of the Spielberg project. Someone of the Dutch television program Zembla of the VARA wanted to know more, and because my cousin Nico refused to cooperate, they approached me. In the end the program never materialized, but what they did want to find out was if the painting concerned a masculine or feminine portrait, and how the transfer with the Germans actually took place. In any case it involved one single painting.

I must say that my uncle Bij already had plans to leave, even before uncle Nathan left for Switzerland. The fact that his profession as an art dealer would help him do so, he did realize. But he had to proceed with caution. The Dutch government in exile had forbidden one from selling art to the occupying forces. And also for that reason it mattered that his brother and companion happened to live in neutral Switzerland. What the Katz firm was trading there, did not concern the Dutch law.

Meanwhile we had run out of time and soon we were facing the autumn of 1942. The unrest only increased, and in many small towns Jews were arrested.

From the Avegoor House in Ellecom, which, a year later, was turned into an *Ausbildungslager* by the SS, Jews who had first been arrested, were now deported and sent to work camps. Every single day we could be next. Going into hiding seemed our only option. Fleeing was no longer possible.

How the final preparations took place I don't know. But at a given moment my parents found themselves in the middle of frequent family meetings in villa 'Welgelegen', on the corner of the Prinsenstraat and the Stationsplein, number 10. Arguments for and against went back and forth, and secret phone calls were made between Dieren and Basel.

In the end twenty-five of us could leave. Twenty-five close relatives of Nathan and Benjamin Katz. My parents, my sister, my brother, and I belonged to that fortunate number.

How exactly everything was carried out has never really been clarified. Who negotiated with whom? How did one determine which of us could go and who couldn't? And the painting, the portrait of a man; how would that end up at the, by the Germans determined, destination?

Uncle Bij became our travel guide, but again, who and how many of us could join? Was the number twenty-five something the Germans had stipulated, or is that simply the number we coincidentally ended up with? The first relatives who definitely came were all members of the Katz family themselves. Then came those ones who were related by marriage, and finally the number would include the ones who did not want to go because they were not prepared to leave others behind, like my mother's brother and sister who believed it wouldn't come that far while supposing that our country would soon be liberated. My grandmother argued that she was too old; she could stay with a non-Jewish grandson and his wife, but in 1943 they arrested and transported her to Westerbork. How far the influence of my Swiss uncle reached, was proven by the fact that he still could buy her freedom with yet another painting. She was allowed to return to her family in Dieren and would die just before the end of the war. The rest of the ones who stayed behind disappeared via Westerbork to Bergen-Belsen.

On 20 October 1942 we left for Amsterdam. On Sunday 1 November - the historian Kooger writes - the last meeting of the Jewish community took place in Dieren. A note with a message from Benjamin Katz was read, who had been the chairman since 1919. It said that 'he, because he had to leave the country would have to resign as chairman.' On that particular Sunday most members of the society would see each other for the last time. Soon after the raids would start in the surrounding area.

15. Memories of the Gibraltar Camp

Something I only began to understand much later had to do with the fact that our Caribbean camp life was funded by the United Kingdom, with which the Jamaican authorities were in constant contact. Afterwards, when we had to repay everything we understood that the Dutch government had financed our stay in advance. Yet no one from London ever came to check on us on behalf of the Dutch government. The island was an outward region that practically did not exist.

I have fond memories of the camp in Jamaica, and I can still envision it. Straight through it, from north to south, ran the Gibraltar Road. Recently I read that the camp owed its name to the Mediterranean Rock because refugees from this eponymous British crown colony had been accommodated here. In 1939, the governor of the island, Mister Richards got the request from London to harbor eleven thousand people from Gibraltar who previously had been evacuated to French Morocco. What kind of people it concerned, and why they had to leave, I was never able to figure out. They may have been exiled Spanish republicans. But it was also possible that they were British nationals who, because of the threat of war, had to find a safe haven.

Whatever the case, in October 1940 four thousand people had to be accommodated, and additional room became necessary for another three thousand in a part of the camp which was still under construction. From a document published in the nineties I deduced that many Gibraltarians weren't too happy about Jamaica. They preferred the crown colony, or went into hiding in England after having been shipped there, while they awaited their final evacuation to the Caribbean. Because of the armed operations at sea this implied no small feat, and eventually one also learned that there weren't enough ships available.

In the end only five hundred of them would reach Jamaica, with the result that most of the living space in the camp remained empty.

In the meantime one had made sure that there was electricity, a phone, water, toilets, a hospital, dining rooms, churches, schools, rooms for amusement, a post office, paved streets with lanterns, and sport accommodations.

When we arrived at the camp we heard that other Jewish refugees had also been brought in, mostly from Poland, and other eastern European countries. During the last months of 1941 they had managed to reach Lisbon with a transit visa, which were provided to them in the south of France by consulates of their corresponding countries. They intended to continue travelling from Portugal to North or South America. Yet the Portuguese authorities made it clear that they had to leave their country before 1942. The consulate of the Polish government in exile partly paid for their stay, the other half had been taken care of by the Jewish Joint Distribution Committee. But, one urgently needed permission from London to raise the sails. Unfortunately the British authorities handled the matter reluctantly; they didn't want European immigrants to enter their overseas colonies fearing that they could become a burden.

Ultimately permission was suddenly granted triggered by the fact that the refugees for whom the camp had been intended for never showed up, and by the overcapacity of the barracks. Those circumstances ensured that on 24 January 1942 the first ship could leave the harbor of Lisbon with approximately five hundred and sixty refugees on board. In March a second ship weighed anchor with another sixty-five refugees. However, after departure some passengers awaited a nasty quarantine for the reason that they had, during a stop in Casablanca, caught a contagious disease.

Thanks to the Joint Distribution Committee and the commander of the camp, Mister Ernest Rae, they were well taken care of in a section which would, hence forth, be called Gibraltar Camp II. From there they would occasionally take a look in Kingston, where they were welcomed by the members of a small Jewish community. The local rabbi organized religious services, and took care of kosher meals.

Within the camp one could not complain about whether there was enough space. Some families even had three or four rooms. Their only problem consisted of the fact that they had no access to the local labor market. However, they found enough activities to keep themselves busy and make themselves useful, such as cleaning, or performing repairs. Social life simply continued. There were shops, even a police station, there were weddings and funerals, and parties and scandals.

The Russian and Polish Jews inhabited Camp II, and lived, like us, in wooden barracks on stilts. In the Dutch part we had our own home, the Katz Barrack.

Inside it was barren, apart from the hammocks and mosquito nets; after all, you only used the quarters to sleep in, and the rest of the day you lived outside underneath the hot sun. In every barrack one had installed shower rooms and sinks. We shared our dining room with the Polish citizens, which also meant that we sometimes ate goulash and borsht, or other things we had never heard of before and didn't always like.

On Jamaica my parents realized that they were very privileged; yet, the fact that they never stopped worrying about their relatives at home, made it impossible for them to enjoy their new surroundings. I never realized how distressed they were, and they allowed me to do whatever I wanted. They found it extremely difficult to feel at home in the camp, and refused to make contact with others outside the family. Learning English, for example, didn't even across their mind, and the only person they did become acquainted with on Curaçao, and who they spent time with in his shop, was an optician who had been interested in the Katz family.

From Curaçao it turned out that it was impossible to get an overview of what was happening on the other side of the ocean, or to learn about what had occurred, or could still befall our family in Holland.

For instance, we didn't know anything about my grandmother. Only uncle Bij, who had left Jamaica and travelled to New York, had been in contact with his brother Nathan in Basel. From the Katz store in New York he, as said before in chapter five, financed our stay with a painting he had sent to Curaçao. I already mentioned how he had left for Holland before us. He boarded the first boat that would leave the United States after the war. I think he returned in September, or in October of 1945, one month before we left, because when we arrived in Dieren in November, uncle Bij and his family already lived there. In July 1947 the Katz firm made sure the empty windows of the ruined synagogue were filled once again.

16. Uncle Benjamin

This book is dedicated to my uncles Nathan and Benjamin, however, after the war some events tarnished their reputation. I even deduced from an article written in 1998 that at the time their actions were open to criticism. They would have sold paintings to Germans, but not only to save us from the concentration camps. The reproach read that, as collaborators, they were guilty of fraud. At the end of the forties my uncle Benjamin had been arrested and spent ten days in prison with someone called Mister de Vries, who, after the war, had been responsible for the return of Dutch paintings from Germany, and returning them to their rightful Dutch owners. However, de Vries never acted disinterestedly, because he only did it for his own advantage. It is important to emphasize here that the painting that had bought our freedom, supposedly never belonged to the Katz brothers. Did they own it in consignation? The same would also apply to all the other paintings the Germans had bought from them.

The case that caught the press' attention was as follows: My uncle Benjamin claimed thirty one paintings after the war, of which a number he and his brother had sold to Alois Miedl. My uncle Nathan, who got twenty-eight paintings back in Switzerland in 1945 or 1946, would have sold over more than one hundred to the Germans, which, according to critical researchers, had happened on a voluntary basis. That is why the request for their return reinforced by the fact that the sale would have occurred under pressure, was invalid. Uncle Benjamin's request would have been submitted without the corresponding invoices from which it would become evident how much was paid for the paintings at the time. Well, unfortunately a lot of the administration of the Jewish art dealers vanished during the German occupation. My uncle had, as they stated, cheated with false invoices and low numbers, and got help from the director of the Dutch foundation of Art Collections, the previously mentioned Dr. Arie Bob de Vries, who also functioned as museum director of the Mauritshuis in The Hague. In 1948 they arrested the director and my uncle, but in the end the case was dismissed after which they were free to leave. I will discuss more details later on.

My uncle Benjamin could not cope with the shame. His arrest led to a deep depression. Yet, he had saved twenty-five people, shouldn't that be prioritized? The Katz art trade had enjoyed Royal protection before and after the war.

However, this affair quickly put an end to it, which also meant the loss of honor. Fortunately, before his death they rehabilitated him.

In 1957 they honored him for his fifty year anniversary, with an exhibition of old paintings from the art trade, and from private collections in the rooms of the Spoorstraat 33-37 in Dieren. On the front of the catalogue he is portrayed with a painting in his hands, the image of Madonna with child.

Five years later, in 1962, he died of a heart attack. He was seventy-one years old.

17. The Aftermath of the War, and the Great Silence

My uncle's case wasn't an isolated incident. As a consequence of all kinds of research one questioned the reputations of many alleged war heroes. Who were initially considered to be models for courage, turned out to be collaborators. The zeitgeist of the nineties asked for a reevaluation of the practices during the years of occupation. One had enough of resistance stories and needed human proportions. After the smoke of the war had been lifted and the major events had found their place in history, a number of special cases surfaced after which one decided to dive into private lives. Nowadays, even in times to come, things are seen in a different light once again, now that, for instance, the post-war reception of returnees from the concentration camps began to be called into question. How did one welcome the survivors in the Netherlands? During the first decades following the war nobody had actually paid attention to this matter. Today one claims that those who had housed Jews weren't as selfless as was initially believed.

I know several cases of persons who suffered greatly during this period, and had to pay a lot for it. With help of resistance groups one had ensured ways of finding hiding places.

However, the resistance never knew for sure how reliable those places were.

Some might have saved lives, but you could ask yourself what that meant for those who had actually gone into hiding. The persons who offered shelter and protection to Anne Frank's family might have been very altruistic, but so many others weren't. Of course there were people who helped because they really wanted to, who felt that because of their religious background it was obvious to take care of the Jews, especially in the reformed circles. There were many Jewish children who had been placed with reformed foster families; children whose parents were deported to the camps. From my immediate environment I know a man who as a baby ended up with strangers at the station as his parents were put on the train to Westerbork. I know that he fared very well with them, which shows that in this case help came from unselfish outsiders, who often had large families.

Recently we see the publication of many stories about how one dealt with the Jews after their return to Holland. We of course were very lucky since we had never known the miseries of the concentration camps. Even so, there were many others who had to start from scratch when they came back. There was nothing. Most of them felt it as very confronting to suddenly take action. The fact alone that something was asked of them, emotionally or materialistically, was already too much. Lately these comments emerge and suddenly one discovers that the Dutch government did little back then. That is one of the reasons why many Jews decided to emigrate to Israel. If there was no one left, and you felt lost in between everyone in Holland, you could at least start fresh there, amidst others who had suffered from a similar tragedy. At least there you were close to the people who had experienced the same, even if you still couldn't really share your story.

However, for us, as previously mentioned, everything turned out to be extremely favorable. I did worry about that fact, especially as I got older. I already mentioned that I did not want to share how I had survived the war. Besides, one at school never asked me about it, even though they knew I was Jewish. The HBS in Arnhem counted four hundred students, and I was the only Jewish boy there. All the other Jewish children who had lived in Dieren, and surrounding areas before the war, never returned. The ones who had survived moved to Amsterdam and other large cities that housed more survivors than in the provinces. I was fifteen or sixteen years old when I started at the HBS. The guilt I felt later on, after we had gone from Dieren to Amsterdam in the fifties and met other Jews. That is where I started working. Initially I lived there with my mother and my brother. My sister had returned from the Indies to Amsterdam, and had bought a house there. We were able to sell our large old villa in Dieren, and find a house in the Maxwellstraat in Amsterdam, close to the one of my sister and brother-in-law.

The person who most of all mattered to me was my uncle Simon Katz, my mother's youngest brother. He could have gone with us to Jamaica, but he thought he would survive in Dieren. Still, later he, his wife and daughter were taken after he had paid a considerable amount of money to provide his family members with hiding places. In hindsight it turned out that all of them were sent from home to home and were barely fed; in short, they experienced a very unpleasant hiding period.

I always felt that uncle Simon was a very sensitive man, a businessman and also an art dealer, who had emerged from the camp being quite sick and mentally ill. After the war I visited his house frequently, at my aunts, my mother's sister-in-law. Their daughter was about my age. At that time, when I was still living in Dieren, they found a house in Arnhem. And there I noticed how my uncle had changed mentally. He constantly suffered from a headache. I had known him from before 1940, before the years of the occupation had turned him into a different person. Initially he gave you the impression to be a charming, nice, and happy man; he was four years younger than my mother. That is how I knew him as a child. After 1945 we always had to look out for him because uncle Simon suffered from a lot of migraines. Neurologists and nerve doctors prescribed a specific medicine with the hope to cure him. His condition really scared me because it made me realize how vulnerable a man can be. What he actually went through remains a mystery to me. One simply never touched his case. My aunt survived him for quite some time; she was eighty years old when she passed away. However, she also never referred to the past. The only thing she ever brought up were the people she knew here in Amsterdam, the ones who had also been sent to the camp. She died without ever talking about what actually had happened. The only explanation I, in her case, can give is that by being silent she was capable to move on with her own life. By shutting out the past she could look forward. Yet, she mostly loved to live in the present.

It happened to be around the same time that I was enlisted. I had been approved but with the help of a befriended doctor who I met in Amsterdam, they fortunately never obliged me to go to the army. He evaluated my situation based on my mother's illness. Through him I was re-inspected, after which they disapproved of me. It must have been the so called factor S5, which stood for mental instability. The idea that I would not have to go under arms was a great relief. However, because of my being disapproved, my brother Jacques, who was four years younger, had to replace me. From Arnhem he had gone to the Handelsschool in Amsterdam, yet he did not manage to finish it. He couldn't evade military service, but it never really bothered him. After all, his service years weren't that difficult; they even allowed him to stay in Amsterdam, which suited me since I really needed his support to deal with my mother's illness. So he was in a position to come home often from the barracks in the Sarphatistraat.

It was in Amsterdam that I became acquainted with Jewish survivors for the first time. I heard how some of them had hold out during the war, but I never felt inclined to bring up my own past.

Later on I noticed, when I had already been married for some time and had children, and after I had become a member of the Liberal Jewish community, and met some of the people my age, that I couldn't talk about my case. It had something to do with that feeling inside of me that said that it didn't matter what had happened to me, which then actually began to surface. Because everyone else had experienced such terrible things. I listened to their stories and heard for the first time how unbelievably horrible it all must have been. For me it brought about ambiguous feelings. On the one hand I always asked myself: why me?

Under normal circumstances I would have never survived the war, and I really admired those who did live through the hardships of the camps. If I had ended up there I wouldn't have made it. I couldn't imagine that I would have hold out such horror. I am not sure why, but I was very unsecure about myself.

18. Assessing my Rescuers

During the final chapters I will have to scrutinize some points of views of others concerning my uncles. A lot has been published about them, and even though this book is merely intended for saying thank you, and honoring them, I can and will not ignore the judgments that have tarnished the way my rescuers acted. Certain things I mentioned earlier in another context, but now I will talk about it in more detail, while taking into account the fact that there are still issues pending of which the decision will be made in the future.

After the great Amsterdam art dealer Jacques Goudstikker had fled to England the Germans raided his house. Initially he had been able to sell his paintings, but for very low prices. His mother, the old Mrs. Goudstikker, decided to stay in Holland. He boarded the ferry from Hoek van Holland to Harwich, but fell from the deck into the hold of the ship. His widow Daisy, an opera singer, was left behind. He only had one son, Edo, who moved to the United States and got married there. Edo's widow, Marei von Saher, the only remaining heir left, started a lawsuit. A lawsuit that had everything to do with what happened after the war. Goudstikker employed several administrators in his enterprise; and what his mother had signed turned out to be a complicated matter.

Since the Goudstikker family had been the first who were plundered by the Germans, my uncles knew what was in store for them. The Goudstikker collection was huge, much larger than the Katz collection. They owned a castle on the banks of the river Vecht, and an outdoor mansion on the river Amstel, named Oostermeer, in addition to a canal house where they traded their paintings. He was one of the largest art dealers in the world. My uncle's business was very small in comparison. The Germans loved art and knew exactly what they wanted. The price one would pay for the paintings during the war was in no way related to their actual value. There were, and still are, trials that discuss this matter.

Shortly after the war had ended, in 1946 and the early days of 1947 my uncles, as mentioned in chapter 16, requested the return of the paintings that had been stolen by the Germans during the occupation or had been forcefully sold for low prices. It is commonly known that uncle Nathan was allowed to move to Switzerland in 1941 in exchange for two paintings; and one year later we, as told at the beginning of my book, left for Spain because of another painting. All this had been published in the newspapers. The painting that bought us our freedom was called in the press 'Portrait of a man of the Raman family'. Supposedly this portrait was handed over to the Germans the moment we set foot on Spanish soil and a phone call of our arrival had been made to Nathan Katz in Switzerland. That is how journalist Adriaan Venema describes it in his book *Kunsthandel in Nederland, 1940-1945.* According to Hans Kooger (*Joods leven in Dieren, Rheden en Velp)* Willy Lages would have called Dr. Hans Posse in Basel from Irun, after which he 'turned his back on the Jews'.

On 11 June 1945 the Foundation for Dutch Art Ownership (FDAO) was established, which, during the same year, managed to retrieve 80% of the art works with museum value that were taken from the Netherlands since 10 May, 1940, and had a combined value of two hundred million guilders. It was something I read in *De Nederlandse Kunstmartkt, 1940-1945* written by Jeroen Euwe. Works of art and art pieces which had been sold on a voluntary basis were now considered to be property of the State. By the end of 1947 the FDAO considered its task to be almost finished.

As such the FDAO (in Dutch the SNK, Sichting Nederlands Kunstbezit) tried to bring back as much art as possible at the expense of the original owners. The historian Gerard Aalders discusses it in *Berooid, de beroofde Joden en het Nederlandse restitutiebeleid* as follows: On 10 December, 1947 the Katz firm received twenty-two paintings from the FDAO, for which, during the war, one would have paid 289.000 guilders. In exchange for that favor the firm offered up two portraits of Heemskerck and Rubens to Dr. de Vries, for the Mauritshuis, which were worth 93.000 guilders in recuperation. Aalders argues that De Vries could have known that Katz sold his paintings freely to Miedl, but De Vries believed it when the Katz firm claimed that most of the money had been given to intermediaries, and according to him the administration of it was destroyed due to the war conditions. De Vries, according to Aalders, was indebted to Nathan Katz because he and his family had also stayed in Switzerland during the war, and had received financial aid. On 9 July, 1948 they arrested Dr. de Vries on suspicion of fraud. The immediate cause was the return of a triptych of Jan van Scorel to the Katz firm that hadn't been stolen, but voluntarily sold. They also arrested Benjamin Katz. De Vries would never regain his post.

In summary, I read that in 1948 the Foundation for Dutch Art Ownership returned thirty-one paintings, among which two Rembrandts, with, at the time, an estimated value of two-and-a-half million guilders to Benjamin Katz in Dieren. For it Katz had submitted a claim to the director of the foundation, Dr. A.B. de Vries. Eight of the thirty-one pieces appeared to be sold to Alois Miedl, the German Verwalter who dealt with the business of the missing Goudstikker. Not Katz, but Miedl, who in the meantime had fled via Spain to Argentina, was the owner. The remaining twenty-three paintings were sold to the Germans by Katz. De Vries had added a clause during the transfer, that, if it were to happen that others could claim the paintings, they would have to be returned to the National Dutch Art Collection (Nederlands Kunstbezit). Some of the paintings seemed to originate from Reichsmarschall Hermann Goering's collection, and from his correspondence we learn that a reasonable amount of money was paid for them.

In a cutout from the *Volkskrant* of 13 July, 1948 I read that both Dr. de Vries and Benjamin Katz were locked up at the Detention Center in The Hague for fraud. The article also mentioned that De Vries was friends with Nathan Katz, who at the time still lived in Basel. Nathan would have helped De Vries after he took refuge in Switzerland during the war.

Two days later *Het Algemeen Handelsblad* publishes an article following the arrest of Dr. de Vries, who was also the director of the Mauritshuis. The article displays a long list of museum directors and renowned art connoisseurs who were shocked when they heard about this matter. They blamed the Justice Department for not having declared the case inadmissible, while citing the merits of Dr. de Vries, and asking for his release. And on 17 July the Council of the Hague Tribunal orders indeed the release of both the director of the Mauritshuis and the art dealer from Dieren (*Het Parool, 17-07-1948*). *De Groene* and *De Waarheid* of 17 and 19 July denounced the imprisonment of Dr. de Vries and Benjamin Katz, besides calling it a shame, and premature, especially when considering the good work done by the first. They protest that nothing proves that the two were to blame for anything.

Two months later, on 16 September, a large article appears in *De Volkskrant* in which I read that Dr. de Vries has been temporarily relieved of his function. The reason is that after the Van Meegeren scandal the Dutch Art Trade had been questioned abroad, and that a public intervention was appropriate. In the article Dr. de Vries is accused of being an accomplice of fraud by Benjamin Katz. Many witnesses assert that they saw the art dealer from Dieren travel to The Hague in a smoking for a rendez-vous with Goering in one of his shops. The Reichsmarschall would have paid reasonable prices for some of the paintings. In addition, he would have ensured that Nathan Katz could freely travel to Switzerland in 1941, where he, concludes the article, one year later met Dr. de Vries. Benjamin Katz, as the article states, was allowed to move to Spain in 1942 because of his German relations.

In *De Volkskrant* Dr. de Vries is questioned since he allegedly postulated that the Katz firm had sold valuable paintings to the Nazis under pressure. However, the Foundation for Dutch Art Ownership never had concrete evidence to support this claim, but nevertheless quickly returned an entire collection to the firm which had voluntarily been sold to the Germans for two million 500.000 guilders. On 2 August 1940, the Katz firm supposedly traded a large number of paintings to Alois Miedl for one million 800.000 guilders. After the war Katz persisted to have been robbed, without ever sending a declaration form, something many others did do. In addition Katz had also done business with Hitler's personal art advisor Dr. Hans Posse, and with Walter Hofer and Martin Bormann, while only the first was mentioned with regards to the announcement that it had happened under duress. The Katz firm corresponded in terms of these matters with the Foundation for Art Ownership via an agent.

Dr. de Vries defended himself during his arrest by saying that he had acted in good faith, but he did admit that the evidence of coercion and sales for low prices were missing. Benjamin Katz had argued that the administration for his art trade had been destroyed in a fire, and that the concrete pieces which could have served as evidence were, as a result, lost. As a settlement he had suggested that the Katz firm would offer a part of the returned collection to the Mauritshuis in The Hague and the Rijksmuseum in Amsterdam. On the other hand, Katz had, in exchange for a landscape painted by Albert Cuyp that hadn't been returned from Germany, received another landscape painted by Albert Cuyp by the foundation as compensation.

Nathan Katz, as one concludes, received unlawfully returned paintings, which despite the ban on the export of art, had ended up in Switzerland. In order to compensate the Katz brothers had donated three valuable paintings to Dutch museums.

On 2 October, 1948 *De Volkskrant* publishes a letter to the editor written by the counselor of the Katz firm, in which the reporter in question of 16 September is accused of acting unlawfully, and a compensation is demanded. In December the case connected to the 'notorious paintings affair where the Dutch state recovered paintings that were sold during the war which were estimated to be worth millions' is suspended by the deputy state lawyer. The recovery had occurred under the responsibility of the deputy state lawyer Mr. de Kempenaar. One speaks of 'corruption of officials'. To that extent the coverage in 1948.

In 1949 Nathan Katz died. During the closing of the criminal investigation against Benjamin Katz and Dr. de Vries, in the spring of 1951, the Minister of Justice considered it to be wise to leave the case alone. The investigation one had started remained in the archives and counted forty-three pages. It discussed the declarations of De Vries, Katz, and numerous witnesses. From it, it becomes evident that the Foundation for Dutch Art Ownership was, according to insiders, a 'corrupt mess'. The museum directors who were a part of the board tried to keep most of the recuperated art to themselves. The result was that the rightful owners of the pieces, who had made claims for restitution had to fight for years in order to get their property back, to finally lose. Their properties were never returned, as they had, in the meantime, been sold at auctions, or had ended up at art dealers or museums. It was theft at state level. The cultural policy objectives tried to keep as much of the national art as possible. Dr. de Vries played an essential role in these politics, but he made an early exception for the Katz brothers. While other claims with better papers ended up in desk drawers, the art dealers from Dieren, The Hague, and Basel were given priority because of friendly relations.

In an article in the weekly *Elsevier* of 1 December, 1973, Eva Katz, Benjamin's daughter, and one of the twenty-five survivors says that even though the Germans came to visit the Katz brothers to buy their paintings, it always occurred with worthless money, false promises, and under duress.

In 1986 Adriaan Venema (op.cit.) states that the Katz brothers were collaborators, that they took things too far in dealing with the Germans, to the detriment of Dutch art possession. Anyone who was friends with Alois Miedl, as confirmed by Venema quoting Professor Isaac Lipschits, was 'terribly wrong and couldn't be trusted'.

In the *NRC Handelsblad* of 27 March, 1998 I read, as written by Lien Heyting, how De Vries asked Nathan Katz to acquire one of the last self-portraits of Rembrandt from 1669, which was rightfully owned by the German Jew Ernst Rathenau who had fled to New York in 1938. The painting was brought to the FDAO in 1947 and still hangs in the Mauritshuis, of which De Vries remained director after the case against him was closed. Heyting emphasized that the 'corrupt mess' at the FDAO was covered up in order to protect the Dutch art trade, and the disgraceful refund policy, especially when considering foreign relations. The Dutch tampering with the return of looted paintings would, in international circles, blacken the already damaged reputation of the Netherlands even more.

The fact that not only the Netherlands was guilty of art theft, but, for instance, also the Soviet Union, became known later on.

Where the 'Portrait of a man of the Raman family' painted by Rembrandt ended up immediately after the war is unclear. It had probably been returned to Nathan Katz in Basel from Munich where the Americans had collected a large part of the in Germany confiscated art works, with the intention to restitute them to the legitimate owners. Now it resides in Los Angeles, but the journey to this city is filled with gaps.

19. The Rembrandt Painting

In 1942 the 'Portrait of a man of the Raman family' travelled from the Swiss city of Basel to the Austrian city of Linz. According to Hans Kooger (op.cit) Dr. Hans Posse wanted to give this portrait to the Führer, with its female counterpart Haesje Cleyburgh, which in 1942 was still hanging in a museum in Dresden. In addition, Benjamin Katz supposedly promised the Germans to buy as much seventeenth and eighteenth century masters as possible, in order to deliver them to the German authorities, according to the previously mentioned article in the weekly magazine *Elsevier* from 1973. He would have tried to keep the Germans on a leash in order to save more people. However, according to Adriaan Venema, author of the book *Kunsthandel in Nederland, 1940-1945* the Katz brothers had provided their services to the enemy, and, in doing so, severely damaged Dutch cultural heritage. The trades made between the Katz firm and the Germans are accompanied by many questions. Did it occur freely, or under duress?

The continuously resurfacing of the never specified 'Portrait of a man of the Raman family' has given luster to Hitler's so-called Hero Gallery in (the Austrian) Linz. Here it could be admired between the end of 1942 and mid-1945. The museum that houses it today stated in 2000, through its assistant vice president of communications and marketing Keith McKeown that an investigation is carried out in order to determine the details of the Raman family. The only thing he knew was that this particular painting had saved twenty-five lives.

We see the bust of a man, slightly turned to the right, facing us. He is wearing a black hat with a wide rim, and a Spanish white collar. His dark clothes do not betray any details. Light is coming in from the left, and his figure throws a vague shadow to the right. The man is wearing a grey beard, his mustache is slightly curly, only his right ear is visible and stands out, and he is looking us straight in the face. It is a portrait of Dirck Janszoon Pesser, painted by Rembrandt van Rijn. It can be seen in the Los Angeles County Museum of Art.

Dirck Janszoon was the son of beer brewer Jan Dammasz Pesser, the owner of De Wittte Leeuw at the Schiedamse Dijk in Rotterdam. In 1612 he married Haesje Jacobs van Cleyburgh. In 1619 his older brother established De Zwarte Leeuw in the Wijnstraat. In 1634 Dirck posed for the painter from Amsterdam, who had specially come to Rotterdam to work on his portrait.

Until around 1650 Rotterdam counted, on average, thirty beer breweries, and their brands were nationally known because of their good taste; the quality of the surface water of the river Maas strongly contributed to this. In Rotterdam one also witnessed, aside from the demand of local citizens, an increase in demand for beer as a result of the growing number of fishing boats and merchant ships.

Dirck Janszoon's parents belonged to the Remonstrants, a community of liberal Protestants. They had been prosecuted by the puritan Synod of Dordrecht, but escaped persecution. Rembrandt didn't only paint Dirck's portrait, but also that of his wife Haesje. Her portrait, which hung in the Los Angeles County Museum of Art too, was acquired in 1985 by the Rijksmuseum in Amsterdam. The country's experts hailed the purchase as a unique opportunity. When initially enough money wasn't available, a public action came to its rescue. With the help of the national television a sponsor show of the BankGiro Lottery would resolve the problem, were it not that at the last moment a strike prevented the broadcast. Eventually the Minister of Culture doubled the government contribution. Haesje cost eleven million guilders.

The portrait of Dirck Janszoon Pesser had once hung at the country seat of Schoonoord at Rijswijk in the eighteenth century, and was owned by Baron Solomon Johan van Gerssdorf, a retired lieutenant colonel of the Utrecht Army. At the onset of the nineteenth century it ended up in Frankfurt am Main, by way of the Parisian art trade, after which, through a certain A. de Ridder, it reached Nathan Katz in Dieren. How and when from there it would emerge in Basel, I have never been able to figure out. It would be interesting to uncover how, after the war, it left Basel and became the possession of the New York art dealer Julius Weitzner. We can assume, as previously mentioned, that Nathan retrieved the painting in 1945, and that it ended up in Switzerland. However, how long it stayed there is unclear. Did it travel straight to New York afterwards, or via intermediate stages? So much is clear that from New York the portrait returned to the Netherlands, at the *Kunsthandel* from Amsterdam called P. de Boer. In 1969 it could be seen in a villa in Wassenaar of a Dutch art collector named Kohn from The Hague. The same year it was bought by the Shickman Gallery in New York, and shortly after it arrived in the hands of the Frances and Armand Hammer Purchase Fund in favor of the County Museum of Art in Los Angeles. Here Dirck Janszoon Pesser is waiting to be reunited with his spouse Haesje van Cleyburgh. This would cost the Dutch state at least ten to twelve million euros.

20. The Claims

In 2007 a new bomb goes off in the Katz case. 'Bloodbath threatens for museums due to claim', and 'New claim on German looted art' were some of the headlines that appeared in the press. The heirs of Nathan Katz demanded the return of 227 of their father's paintings which the state had lent to several museums. The Institute Collection of the Netherlands is shaking on its foundations, because this claim exceeds by far the value of the one the descendants of the Goudstikker's made several years earlier. And their case turned out to be successful in 2006 after almost ten years of haggling. So the Katz family must have felt it was time to take action. Again the question raises whether the artworks had indeed been sold voluntarily, or under pressure, to the Germans. Historian Gerard Aalders, author of the book *Roof, de ontvreemding van Joods bezit tijdens de Tweede Wereldoorlog,* and associated with the Dutch Institute for War Documentation (NIOD in Dutch), calls the claim dubious. In a magazine of the government *PM*, he argues that 'those transactions were made under normal market prices. Katz traded on a large scale, and entirely voluntarily with the occupying forces.' However, the Restitution Committee objected in 2005: 'considering the questionable reputation of Miedl it cannot be excluded that the sale had been completely involuntarily.' In addition, it is well known that both Nathan and Benjamin used paintings to ensure a safe haven for themselves and their families.

The claim for 227 paintings of the Katz family at the Dutch State was submitted by Sybilla Katz Goldstein from Florida (USA), daughter of Nathan Katz. Her New York attorney Tina Talarchyk emphasizes the involuntary nature of the sales. The government minister Ronald Plasterk has asked the Restitution Committee to investigate the legality of the claim. Among the works are those hanging in nothing less than the Museum De Lakenhal in Leiden, the Frans Hals Museum in Haarlem, the Mauritshuis in The Hague, and the Rijksmuseum in Amsterdam.

Aside from Sybilla, two other sisters Margarethe and Eva, in addition to her brother David Katz, did join the claim. David Katz is living in Basel, and stated in a phone call to the *NRC Handelsblad* of 24 September, 2007, that it concerns even more than 227 paintings. The Goudstikker case taught David Katz that the Dutch State is not really cooperative, and he expects that the demand of the Katz family will be prolonged until he, eighty-eight years old, and his elderly sister are dead. He knows for sure that his father sold the paintings under duress: 'If you didn't sell, a gun would be put to your head, or you would be deported to a camp.'

Once in a while David Katz returns to the Netherlands, to relive some of the old memories in Dieren and Arnhem. Among other things he, according to the newspaper, would have said that the blazon of his father Nathan threatened to be smeared as a consequence of a faulty declaration made by his brother. Because Benjamin reported amounts that were much less than what the Germans supposedly paid (*Het Parool,* 25 September). At the time twenty-eight works had been returned to Benjamin, but for it he had submitted invoices with numbers that were a lot lower than what he had gotten for it. In contrast, Nathan Katz was reputed to be generous in Switzerland by financially helping Dutch refugees and stateless individuals, as became evident from letters of the Dutch embassy in Bern.

Therefore, Nathan, unlike Benjamin couldn't be blamed for any of it. However, the statement made by his oldest son David from Switzerland, as a consequence of the claim, brings forward a possible disagreement between Nathan and Benjamin, or at least between both of their heirs.

Once the brothers had been extremely successful due to their exceptional collection. During the war they made a lot of money with their sales, historian Helen Schretlen repeats, also the co-author of the book *Betwist bezit. Stichting Nederlands Kunstbezit en de teruggave van roofkunst na 1945*. However, the question is whether they sold all the paintings for personal financial gain, or because they did it to save their own lives. Outspokenly sharp is columnist J.A.A van Doorn in the newpaper *Trouw* of 6 October, 2007. Under the head of 'Predatory art attracts vultures' he calls the brothers Nathan and Benjamin Katz 'vulgar collaborators', who attacked Dutch Art Ownership.

In the thirties Miedl had moved to the Netherlands. 'Many more Jews did business with him, especially during the first year of the war,' declares Rudi Ekkart, director of the National Office for the Documentation of Historic Art. A committee under the leadership of Ekkart established the rules for the restitution of looted art some years ago. He is also the head of the

Origins Unknown Agency which inventoried thousands of stolen works. However, despite the fact that he sold many works to the German authorities, Miedl wasn't really considered to be an exponent of the German regime. He was an extraordinarily keen, charming art dealer, according to Ronnie Naftaniël, director of the Center of Information and Documentation Israel (CIDI), who states: 'He always said: "Sell your art now, because soon you will not get a penny for it." And he paid one good money.' The Jewish art dealers in Holland knew what had happened to their German colleagues, according to Naftaniël, who is also associated with the Origins Unknown Agency. 'They had lost many of their art to the Nazi regime. They knew: we need to get rid of our trade before it is taken from us, even if we have to sell to the Germans.'

The works sold to Miedl by the Katz brothers have, in several publications, always been regarded as deliberate actions. The fact that the relationship between Miedl and Nathan Katz became better and better, certainly contributed to that fact. In the spring of 1941 Miedl would have spent the night at Nathan Katz' house in Arnhem. And the relationship with Hans Posse was also good. According to Emeritus Professor Isaac Lipschits there is no room for doubts: 'Anyone befriended with Miedl during the war, must be considered as completely wrong, and couldn't be trusted. Miedl could not be taken for a regular art dealer, he was simply Goering's buyer.' Yet, according to the previously cited Eva Katz, Benjamin's daughter, there was no such thing as a voluntary sale, as the above mentioned interview in *Elsevier* in 1973 makes clear: 'The Germans supposedly visited my father's business to buy paintings, sometimes they paid, sometimes they didn't, with worthless money, or false promises of later payments. My father's optimism decreased and then he would stare out the window for hours, as if somewhere in the distance there loomed hope for survival and a good outcome.'

At first glance it appears that the claim made by the heirs of the Katz family has little chance to succeed. Nonetheless: we do not know for sure if the brothers dealt with the Germans on a voluntary basis. And from earlier statements made by the Restitution Committee it is also evident that Miedl put a lot of pressure on other sellers. However, the point is that the claim lacks a sound basis. Of a substantial number of the 227 paintings one can already establish that they do not meet the conditions for return. Besides, it appears now that a number of them had already been merchandised before the war and that many of them weren't even sold to the Germans, but to Dutch art dealers and individual buyers.

21. Forced Sale, or Voluntary Trade?

Already since 1994 my family had envisaged the plan, especially under the influence of my cousin David Katz in Switzerland, and his sister Sybilla who was living in New York at the time. In 2000 their project came to life. In 2003 Nathan Katz' children submitted a claim for one piece of art as a test case. The same year they hold the Swiss State accountable for a Rembrandt painting that Nathan Katz had been forced to give to the Germans in order to save his mother from Westerbork.

Sybilla always maintained that many of the art works were stolen by the Germans from her father's villa in Arnhem, after they had left for Switzerland. The art collection covers both brothers, both her father Nathan, and her and my uncle Benjamin. Now she demands that those pieces are returned to her. The Katz family felt they had the right to a refund. Once I visited an exhibition organized by the Restitution Committee in Leeuwarden. The committee was responsible for the return of paintings which were unlawfully obtained by the Germans, like those of the Goudstikker family. And those are today being displayed in several museums. The exhibition also included a large photograph of my uncle Bij.

When my cousin Sybilla and her husband came to Holland they stayed in Amsterdam, at Hotel Krasnapolsky. Unfortunately he is no longer with us today. They were the ones who came up with the idea to take matters into their own hands, and to act. I thought it was nice seeing her again. When visiting them in their hotel I noticed that she wanted to be informed by me in all details. But I wasn't much help, since I knew nothing of what she asked me. The only thing that became clear right from the start was that she demanded that the paintings in question be returned to her. I didn't quite know how many of them she wanted, but in hindsight I realize I was quite naïve at the time. She merely needed me for information, however, it wasn't my world of expertise. My mother wasn't a legal heiress, so we never really cared for those paintings. And after the war the matter did not interest me. Everything I knew I told her. Later on it turned out, when she had returned to the United States, that a claim had been submitted to the Ministry of the Arts and Sciences, a claim that required the return of several hundred paintings. In 2007 they hired lawyers because they were encouraged by the success of the Goudstikker case. Yet after presenting such a request one would have to wait until all the subsequent research came to an end. And the details had everything to do with my uncle Nathan.

In the meantime my oldest cousin Nico, the only son of my uncle Benjamin who lived in the Netherlands, passed away in 2006. And he was the only one who had children, and they were told that their cousins and nephew, the children of their uncle Nathan, had requested the return of the paintings. As a consequence Nico's children all became involved in the case. So it mostly concerns the grandchildren of my uncle Benjamin.

The painting that saved our lives is one I never got the opportunity to see. My family ignored the subject. Only one of my cousins, a grandson of uncle Bij did see it. I remember that it was sold in Wassenaar. And my cousin travelled to Los Angeles to admire it in the County Museum, where he made some photographs of it. Those are placed on the website katz.nl

Why of all paintings did Dr. Posse want this one? Perhaps because at the time it happened to be the only Rembrandt owned by Nathan. How it fared after the war, as mentioned in an earlier chapter is something I do not know. And how it got to end up in the hands of Mr. Kohn in Wassenaar remains a mystery.

Recently two of my grandnieces visited me from the United States. They live in Florida, and also decided to submit a claim. They are the granddaughters of my uncle Bram from Apeldoorn. Like Nathan and Benjamin, Bram worked as an art dealer as well, and their mutual contacts were intensive. These women also demanded the return of the paintings that once belonged to their grandfather, and since uncle Bram was my mother's brother, I and my children became involved in the cause. However, the basis for it was unstable.

The simple fact is that Benjamin and Nathan did not leave behind a will, and that is the main reason why my grandnieces decided to submit a claim as a third party. They hired a Dutch lawyer.

Forced sale or involuntary trade? That is the question for those involved. The Restitution Committee under the leadership of Rudi Ekkart now believes that the paintings were willingly and freely sold to the Nazis. But how can one say such a thing when the Jews knew what could happen to them, while knowing that time was running out? How much time would they have left? Perhaps, under normal circumstances, they would have preferred to keep their paintings.

However, the plaintiffs state it differently. Sybilla Goldstein Katz asks for a refund from the Swiss government in a letter written on 30 January, 2004, alleging that her father and thirty-four others were only allowed to stay in Switzerland in exchange for works of art. In the meantime the claim for thirty-one pieces has been rejected, based on the fact that the inventory of the Katz firm had gone missing, and because Katz also sold their paintings as a loan.

Sybilla Katz told us that most of the possible profits – she talks about 1.25 billion dollars – would be made available to the surviving victims of the Holocaust. But, how many of them are still alive? Moreover, Swiss banks are asking for supporting documents, death certificates etc. The Rembrandt that saved our lives, the portrait of Dirck Janszoon Pesser, is in any case, not a part of any claim. If it had been we would have known from the start. The fact that the portrait of Dirck was returned to Nathan after the war is something we know for sure, as well as the fact that he sold it shortly after. However, what happened to the painting until 1969 is difficult or perhaps even impossible to uncover.

22. Conclusion

As I look back at my past I think that the time between my tenth and thirteenth year was like the spring of my life. During my stay on Jamaica and Curaçao I experienced the essential things that greatly influenced the course of my days to come. New friends, a new language (English, Spanish), music, climate, it all enraptured me. I got the opportunity to soak it up and enjoy it to the fullest. When those years ended in September 1945, the summer gave way to the beginning of winter, while being back in a country that had been damaged because of the war. The culture shock I endured was overwhelming, and deeply disappointing was the reception in our village by the ones who assumed they would never see us again. The loss of my father due to his illness, and that of my grandparents and aunts who never returned from Auschwitz, Bergen-Belsen made it appear as if the winter would last forever. When I, some years later decided to go to secondary school in Arnhem things were looking up for me for a short time, with new friends, with the music, and tennis. However, my mother's illness interrupted my relief and made things more difficult once again.

Looking back at my life, at the last seventy years, I am well aware of the fact that without my uncle's transaction I probably wouldn't have survived the war, or would have returned heavily traumatized. Hence this testimony has to make it absolutely clear that the Rembrandt deal saved the lives of twenty-five people!

This book is a homage to Benjamin and Nathan Katz. It is very regrettable that my family, all heirs of my grandfather David Katz, argue about a claim that revolves around whether the paintings were stolen or not. I hope that I, in my remaining years may enjoy the company of my children, grandchildren, partners and friends. One of the things I recently got to participate in was the Bar Mitzvah of my sweet little grandson Noah, on 17 November, 2011. It happened to be the fourth time that our family assisted at a Bar Mitzvah, after the one I had in 1945 in Willemstad, the one of my son Dennis in 1977 in Amsterdam, and that of Imri in 1999 in Kfar-Saba. Noah's Bar Mitzvah took place in a beautiful synagogue and the singing of his Parsha sounded like music to my ears. I expect to be present at Sem's Bar Mitzvah in the near future too. New faces bring hope and dreams to the lives of the elderly.

One detail that continues to intrigue me is the family portrait that was taken of the twenty-five of us by the Germans at the Spanish border, the one that also included Ferdinand Aus der Fünten and Willy Lages. Whether that portrait was meant to be used as propaganda, or if it was a piece of evidence for the exchange, I cannot tell you. Perhaps the Germans wanted to prove that they weren't as bad as people said they were because they had saved the lives of twenty-five Jews. We never saw that photo, and in the Netherlands it did not come to the surface. An enquiry at Yad Vashem in Israel, the Holocaust Memorial Museum in Washington, and the Bundesarchiv in Berlin never led to anything. I guess that photograph is placed somewhere in an unknown archive gathering dust.

Epilogue

On January 2013 the Restitution Committee announced that the claim submitted by the Katz family had been rejected. Of the 189 paintings in question only one could be considered as a painting once owned by the Katz brothers which they were supposedly forced to sell. This painting hangs in a museum in Gouda.

The negative advice for the 188 paintings from the Katz claim officially states:

The Hague, 24 January, 2013 – the Advisory Restitution Committee for Cultural Goods during the Second World War advises minister Jet Bussemaker of Education, Culture and Science (the OCW) to completely reject the claim for the return of 189 paintings from the National Collection. After research the Committee concludes that the conditions for a refund have not been met. An exception, however, is the portrait of the "Man with the high beret", painted by Ferdinand Bol.

The claim was submitted by 21 descendants of the Jewish brothers Benjamin and Nathan Katz, who, since 1930 owned the Art Trade Firm D. Katz in Dieren. The descendants state that the Katz firm involuntarily lost the 189 requested items, mostly paintings, during the Nazi regime. For this reason they decided to submit this claim in 2007. The Committee examined this case in detail and concludes that practically all the art works do not meet the conditions for a refund. The two main requirements under the applicable policy are that one knew for certain that the Katz firm owned the paintings, and that it is highly likely that the paintings were sold under duress.

188 rejected works of art did not meet one or either of these conditions. The only exception is the portrait of the "Man with the high beret", painted by Ferdinand Bol. The Committee stated, in terms of this painting, that both the ownership condition, and the forced nature of the loss of possession were proven. For that reason the Committee advised minister Bussemaker to return this piece to the descendants of the Katz brothers. The minister has agreed to do so.

It is unclear if, in the future, the family will continue to initiate legal proceedings. However, it is evident that the last word about this matter has not yet been spoken.

Names and Particulars

Casper Izak Cohen x Mina Cohen- Katz
(24-9-1899 — 27-10-1948) (7-11-1899 — 5-3-1958)

– Vrouwtje Wurbik-Cohen x Kurt Georg Wurbik
(30-1-1927— 7-6-2008) (5-4-1922 — 9-5-2006)

– David Cohen x Stephanie Weinbaum
(23-7-1932—) (14-3-1934—)

– Izak Caspar Cohen (Jacques)
(17-3-1936 — 16-2-1986)

Benjamin Katz (1-4-1891
— 14-1-1962)

– Eva Katz
(12-5-1911 — 1995?)

Nathan Katz
(5-8-1893—1949)

– Sybilla Goldstein-Katz
(28-5-1933—)

Bram Katz
(9-1-1897 — 11-12-1984)

– Elia Katz
(12-4-1932—)

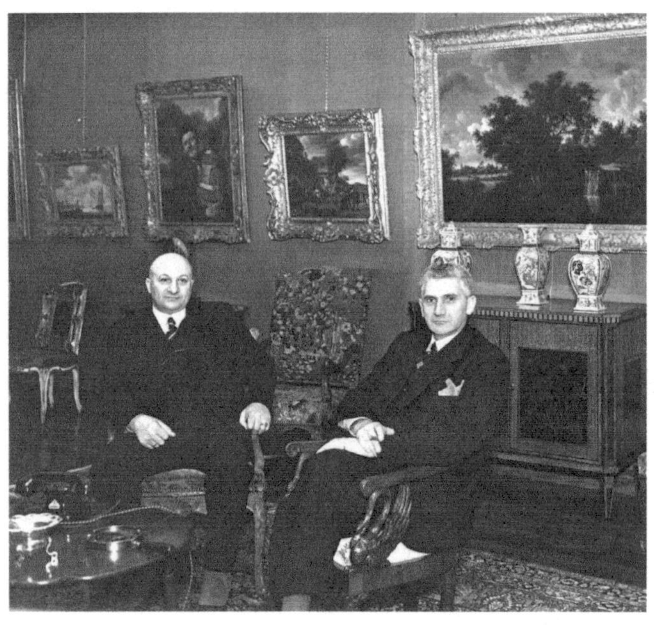

Benjamin and Nathan Katz.

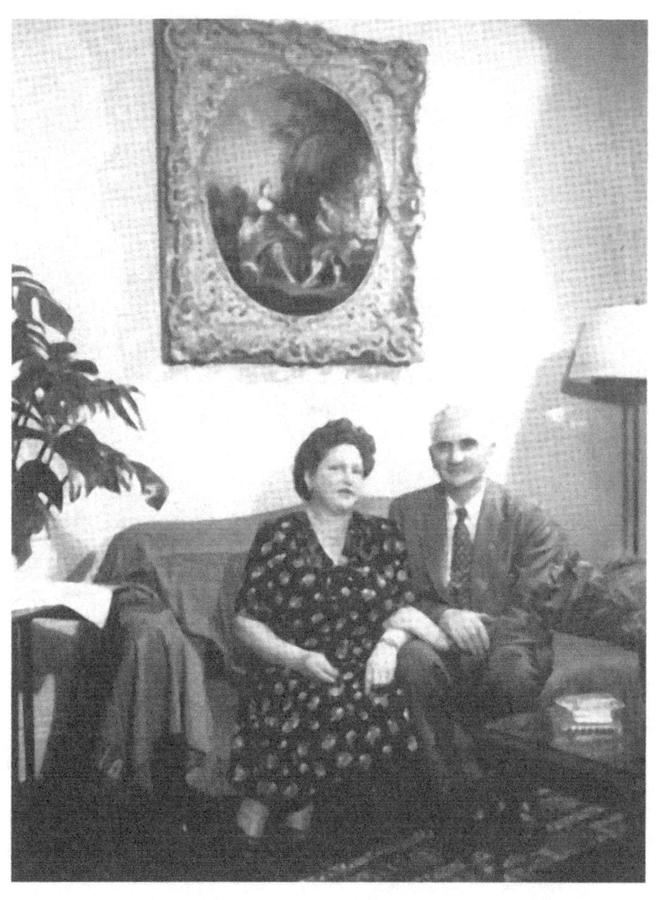

Benjamin Katz and his wife Marianne, New York, 1946.

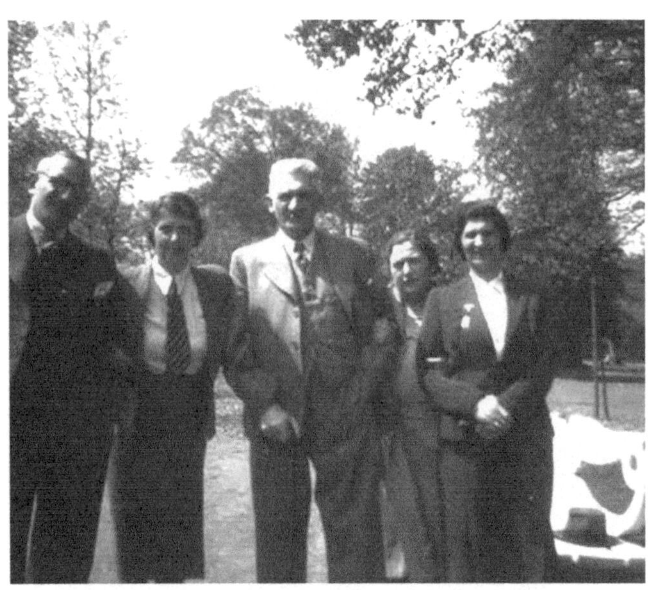

David's father is pictured on the left, in the middle uncle Benjamin, on the right next to him Marianne, and to her right is David's mother.

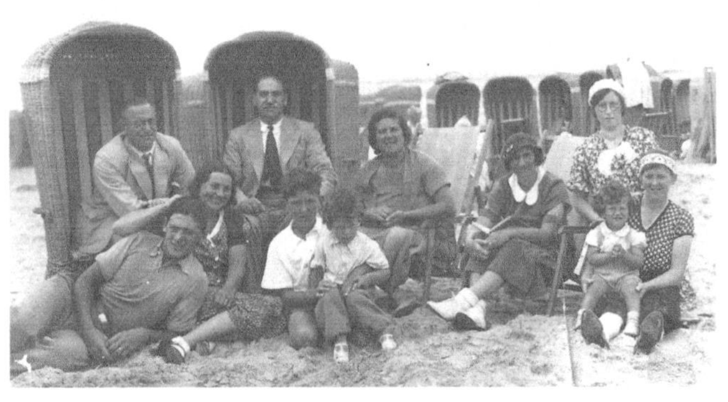

In Zandvoort with on the right David and a nurse.

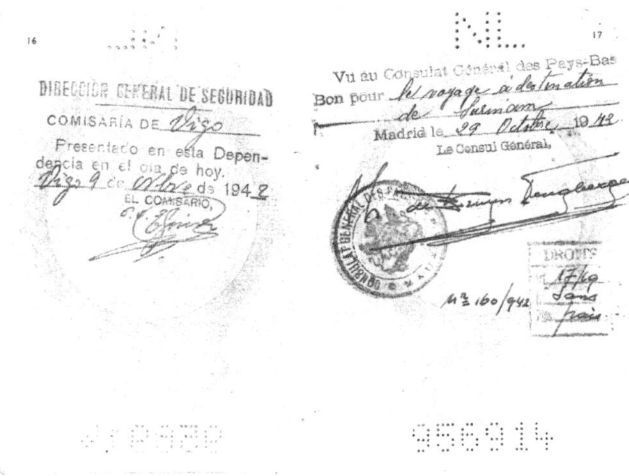

16

DIRECCIÓN GENERAL DE SEGURIDAD
COMISARÍA DE Vigo
Presentado en esta Dependencia en el dia de hoy.
Vigo 9 de Octubre de 1942
EL COMISARIO,

17

Vu au Consulat Général des Pays-Bas
Bon pour le voyage à destination de Surinam
Madrid le 29 Octobre 1942
Le Consul Général,
DROITS
Sans frais

956914

A document for the departure from the port of Vigo at the Marqués de Comillas on 9 October, 1942, and a document that enables one to leave on behalf of the Dutch Consul General in Madrid.

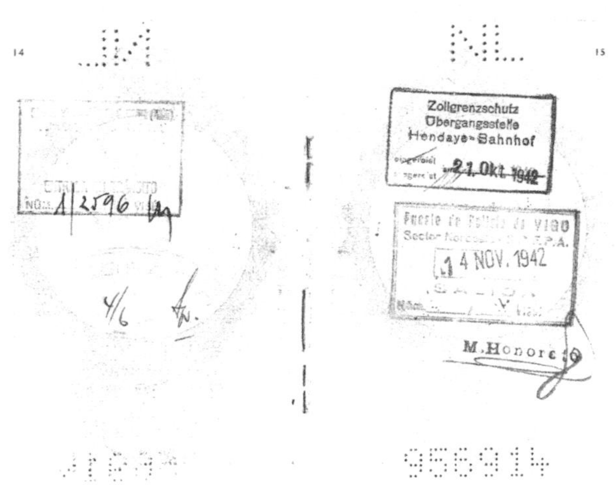

14

NÚM. 1/2596

15

Zollgrenzschutz
Übergangsstelle
Hendaye-Bahnhof
21.Okt.1942

Puesto de Policia de VIGO
14 NOV. 1942

M.Honoré

956914

Documents for crossing the border between France and Spain at Hendaye.

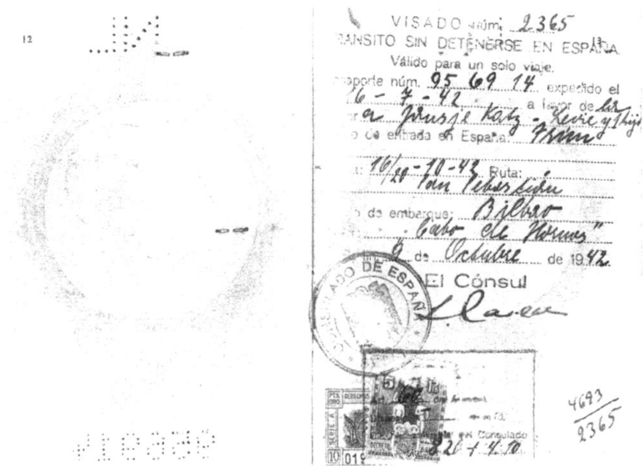
VISADO núm. 2365
ANSITO SIN DETENERSE EN ESPAÑA
Válido para un solo viaje.
saporte núm. 95 69 14 expedido el
6 - 7 - 42 a favor de
de entrada en España: Irún
16/20-10-42 Ruta: San Sebastián
de embarque: Bilbao
"Cabo de Hornos"
9 de Octubre de 1942
El Cónsul

Transit Visa for Spain, given in Bilbao.

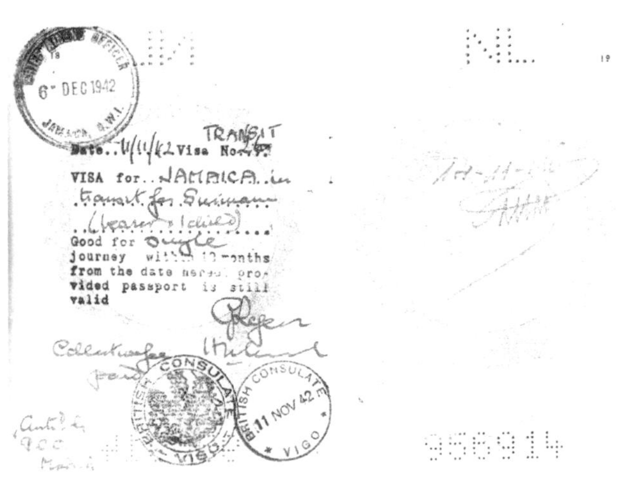
6 DEC 1942
JAMAICA, B.W.I.
TRANSIT
Date..11/11/42 Visa No.
VISA for..JAMAICA..in transit for Surinam
Good for single journey within 12 months from the date hereof provided passport is still valid
BRITISH CONSULATE VIGO
BRITISH CONSULATE 11 NOV 42 VIGO

Transit Visa for Jamaica.

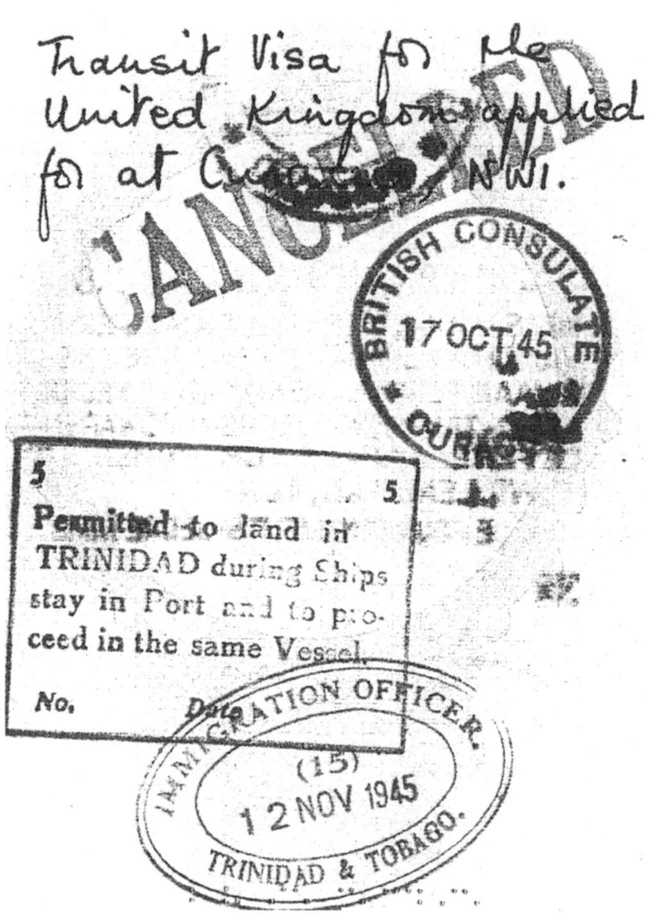

Transit Visa for the
United Kingdom applied
for at Cu[illegible], NWI.

BRITISH CONSULATE
17 OCT 45

5 5
Permitted to land in
TRINIDAD during Ships
stay in Port and to proceed in the same Vessel.
No. Date

IMMIGRATION OFFICER.
(15)
12 NOV 1945
TRINIDAD & TOBAGO.

Documents for a stop in Trinidad.

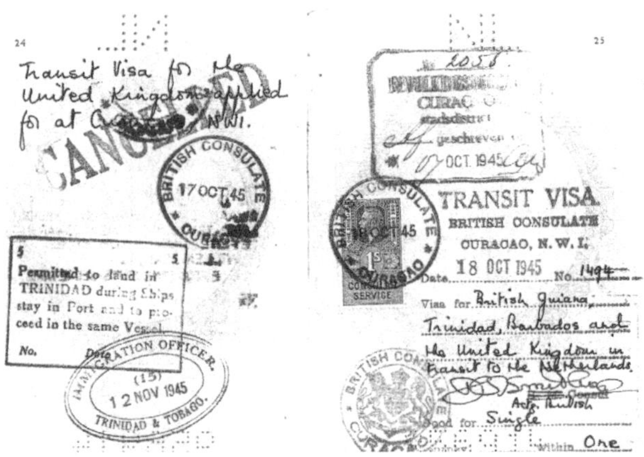

Transit Visa for Trinidad and Curaçao.

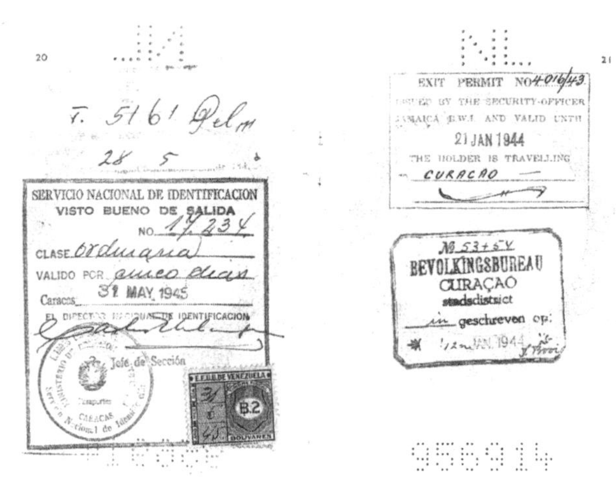

Documents for Venezuela (for David's aunt and sister because of medical treatment) and Curaçao.

22

Houdster van dit paspoort is sedert 7 Januari 1944 gevestigd op Curaçao. Bearer of this passport is domiciled at Curaçao since January 7th 1944.

Curaçao, 12 Februari 1945

VOOR DEN GOUVERNEUR VAN CURAÇAO
DE GOUVERNEMENTS-SECRETARIS
H. Schotborgh

ESTADOS UNIDOS DE VENEZUELA
REGISTRADO
Caracas ..... de ..... de 1.94
28 MAY 1945

23

GOUVERNEMENTS-SECRETARIE
CURAÇAO

GOUVERNEMENT VAN CURAÇAO
NIETS TEN NADEELE VAN DEN HOUDER VAN DIT PASPOORT BEKEND. GEEN BEZWAAR TEGEN BINNENKOMST IN NEDERLAND, TENZIJ INTUSSCHEN BEZWARENDE FEITEN AAN HET LICHT KOMEN.
WILLEMSTAD, den 16 Oct. 1945
DE GOUVERNEMENTS-SECRETARIS,
No 98.

DIENST DER GRENSBEWAKING
AMSTERDAM
29/11 45

Documents supplied in Willemstad.

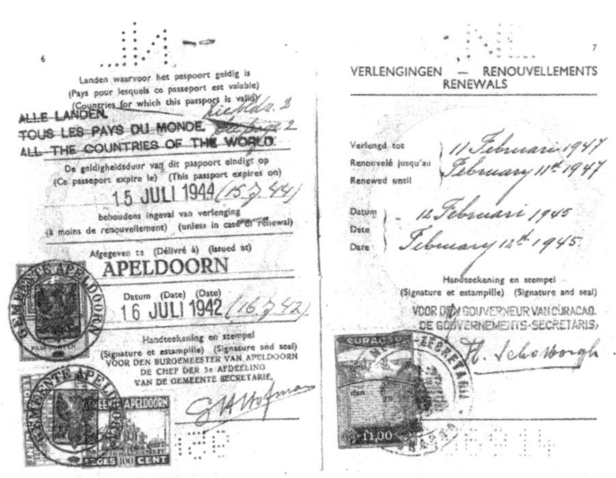

6

Landen waarvoor het paspoort geldig is
(Pays pour lesquels ce passeport est valable)
(Countries for which this passport is valid)

ALLE LANDEN.
TOUS LES PAYS DU MONDE.
ALL THE COUNTRIES OF THE WORLD.

De geldigheidsduur van dit paspoort eindigt op
(Ce passeport expire le) (This passport expires on)
15 JULI 1944 (15-7-44)
behoudens ingeval van verlenging
(à moins de renouvellement) (unless in case of renewal)

Afgegeven te (Délivré à) (Issued at)
APELDOORN

Datum (Date) (Date)
16 JULI 1942 (16-7-42)

Handteekening en stempel
(Signature et estampille) (Signature and seal)
VOOR DEN BURGEMEESTER VAN APELDOORN
DE CHEF DER 3e AFDEELING
VAN DE GEMEENTE SECRETARIE,

GEMEENTE APELDOORN

7

VERLENGINGEN — RENOUVELLEMENTS
RENEWALS

Verlengd tot / Renouvelé jusqu'au / Renewed until: 11 Februari 1947 / February 11th 1947

Datum / Date / Date: 12 Februari 1945 / February 12th 1945

Handteekening en stempel
(Signature et estampille) (Signature and seal)
VOOR DEN GOUVERNEUR VAN CURAÇAO.
DE GOUVERNEMENTS-SECRETARIS,
H. Schotborgh.

CURAÇAO
1,00

Exit Visa for the Katz Family in Apeldoorn.

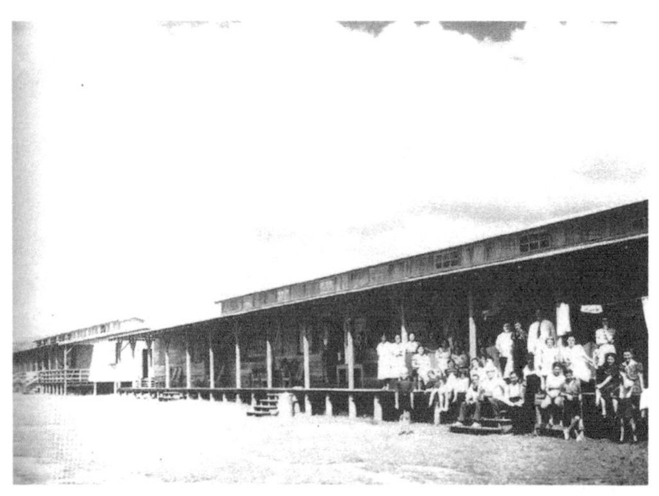

The Gibraltar Camp, Jamaica.

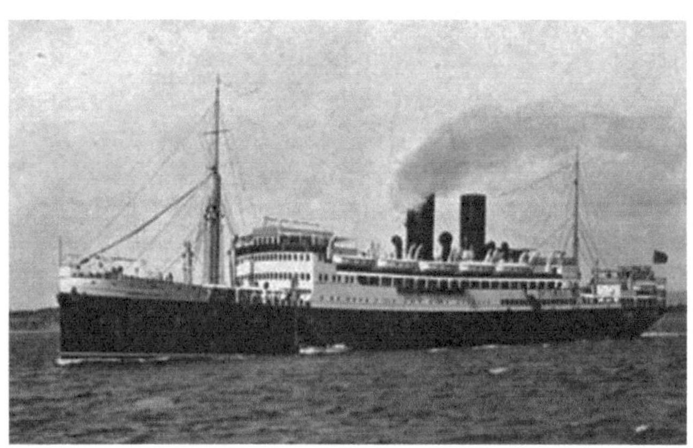

Marqués de Comillas.

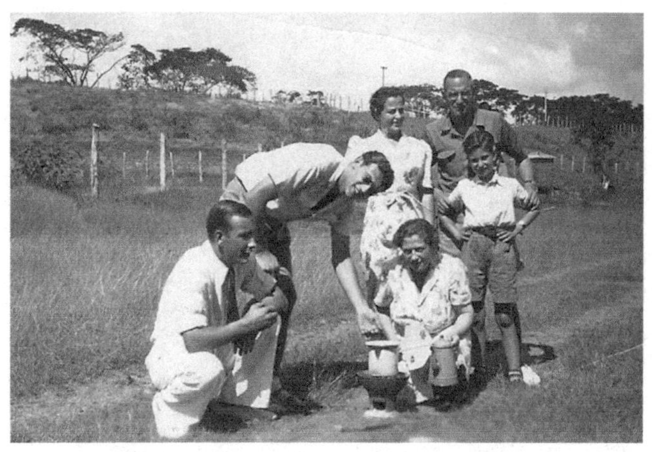

David and his father, Jamaica.

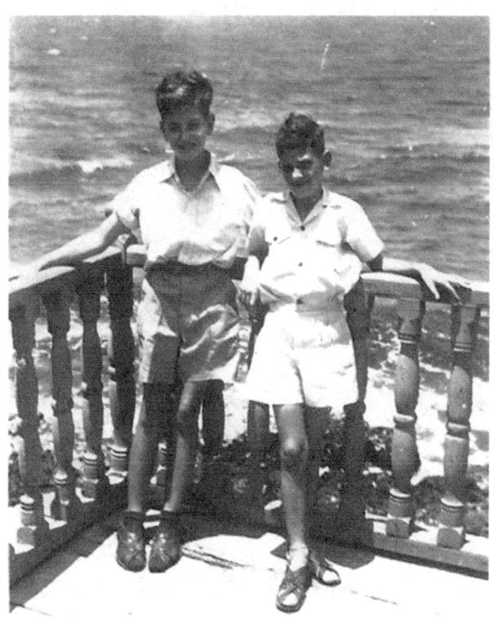

David and his brother Jacques on Curaçao.

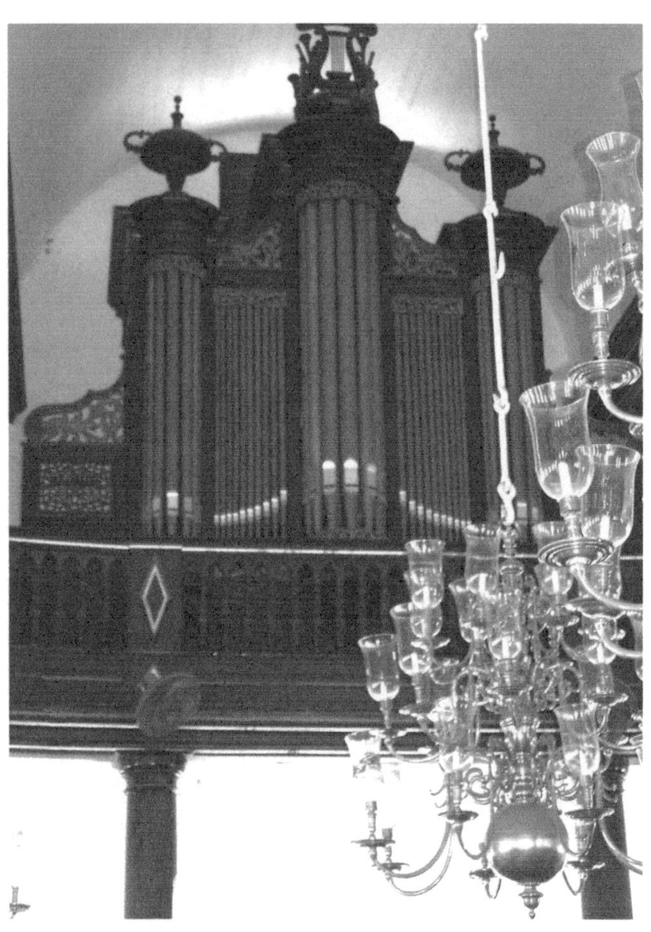

Synagogue, Willemstad.

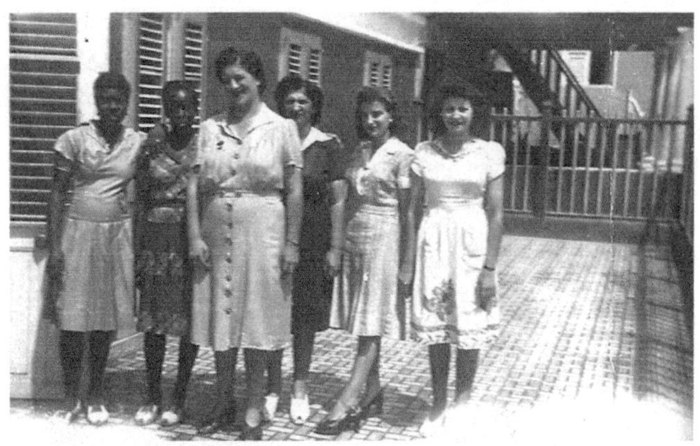

David's sister is pictured on the right, Aunt Jans is pictured the third from the left with immediately behind her David's mother and in between his niece Siny.

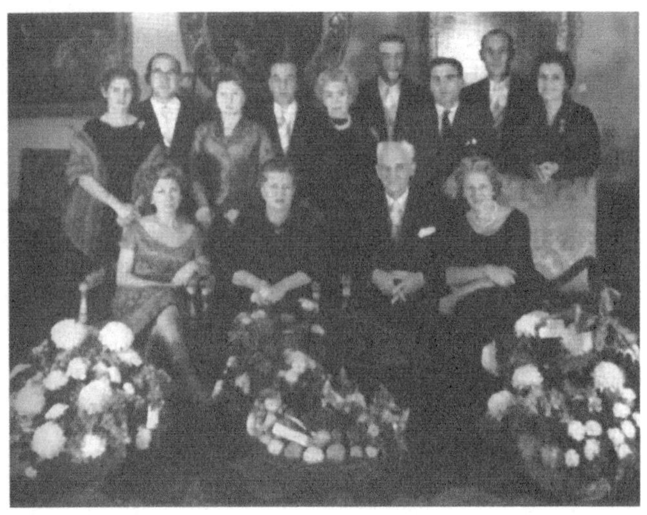

The Katz family, 1957, 50 year anniversary.

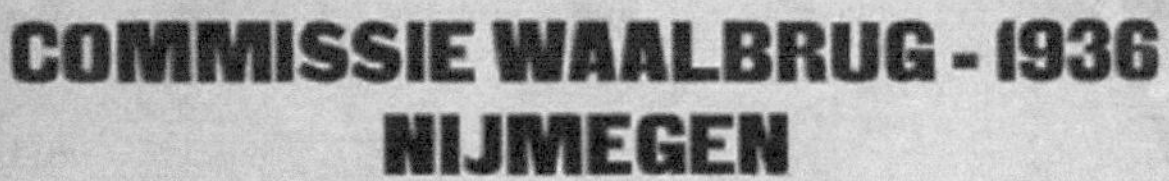

COMMISSIE WAALBRUG - 1936
NIJMEGEN

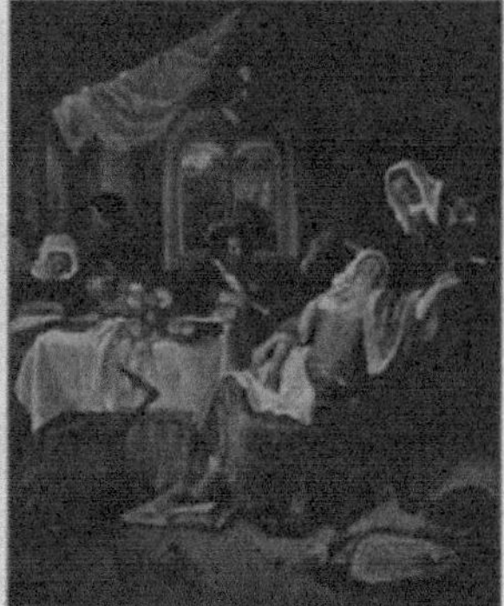

Jan Steen - Vroolijke Huishouding (109 x 92 cM)

TENTOONSTELLING

van 16e en 17e eeuwsche Hollandsche, Vlaamsche en Italiaansche schilderijen (o.a. van Rembrandt, Jan Steen, Joos van Cleef, P. P. Rubens, Lorenzo di Credi) en antiquiteiten uit de collectie der

firma D. KATZ te Dieren

in Huize „Belvoir", Keizer Lodewijkplein (ingang Waalbrug) te Nijmegen

Van 15 Juli tot en met 1 September 1936

Geopend alle werkdagen en ook des Zondags van 10 tot 5 uur
Entree 50 cents, ten bate van de Commissie Waalbrug - 1936

Katz firm exhibition, 1936.

COMMISSIE WAALBRUG - 1936
NIJMEGEN

—

TENTOONSTELLING
VAN 16e EN 17e EEUWSCHE
HOLLANDSCHE, VLAAMSCHE EN
ITALIAANSCHE SCHILDERIJEN
(O.A. VAN REMBRANDT, JAN STEEN, JOOS VAN
CLEVE, P. P. RUBENS, LORENZO DI CREDI) EN

ANTIQUITEITEN

—— UIT DE ——
COLLECTIE DER FA. D. KATZ TE DIEREN

◆

VAN 15 JULI
TOT EN MET 1 SEPTEMBER 1936
IN HUIZE „BELVOIR", KEIZER LODEWIJK-
PLEIN (INGANG WAALBRUG) TE NIJMEGEN

Katz firm exhibition, 1936.

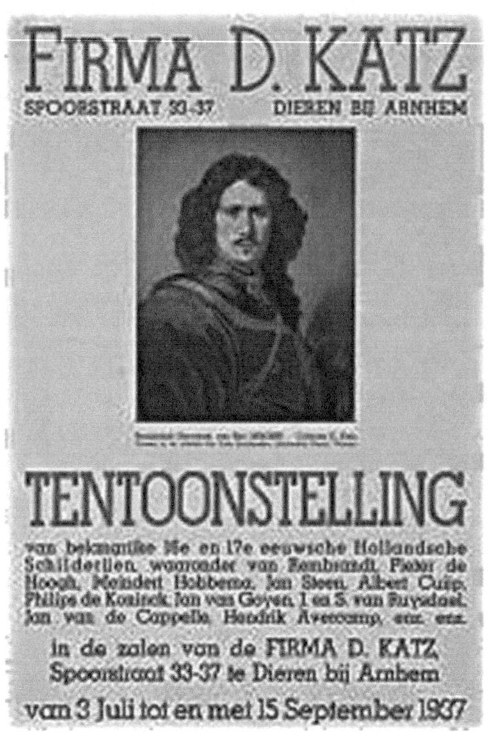

Katz firm exhibition, 1937.

FIRMA D. KATZ

SPOORSTRAAT 33-37, DIEREN BIJ ARNHEM

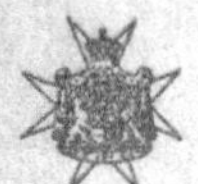

HOFLEVERANCIER VAN WIJLEN Z.K.H. PRINS HENDRIK DER NEDERLANDEN

TENTOONSTELLING

VAN 16DE EN 17DE EEUWSCHE HOLLANDSCHE EN VLAAMSCHE SCHILDERIJEN

WAARONDER VAN REMBRANDT, VAN DIJCK, JAN STEEN, J. EN S. VAN RUYSDAEL, PHILIPS KONINCK, JAN VAN DE CAPPELLE, JAN VAN DER HEYDEN, ENZ. ENZ.

IN DE ZALEN VAN DE MAATSCHAPPIJ „ARTI ET AMICITIAE" ROKIN 112 TE AMSTERDAM

VAN 7 MEI TOT EN MET 4 JUNI 1938

DAGELIJKS, OOK DES ZONDAGS, GEOPEND VAN 10 TOT 18 UUR.

Katz firm exhibition 1938.

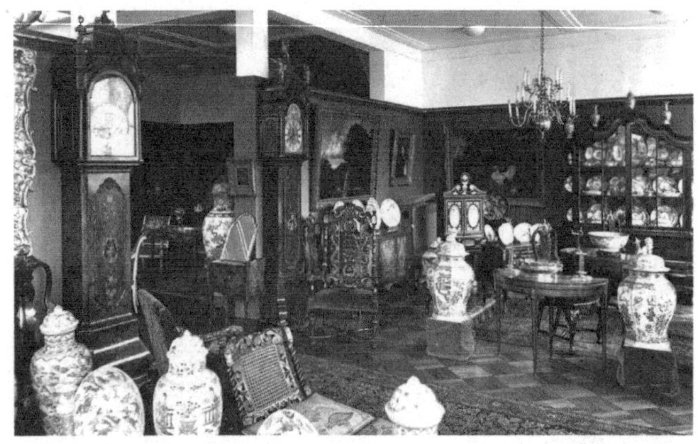

The interior of the Katz Art Store.

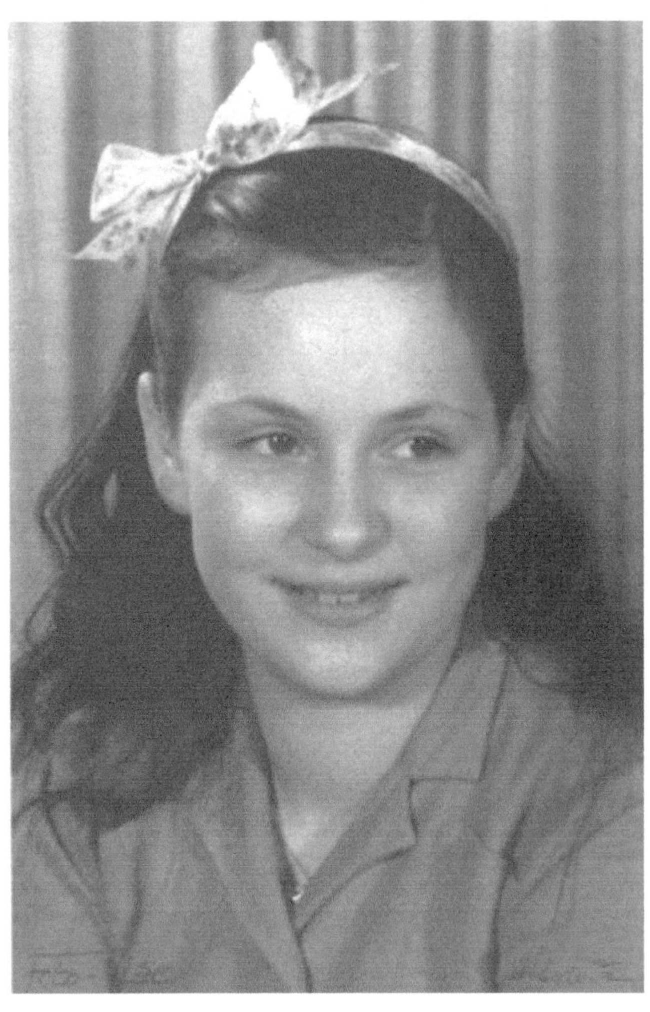

Steffi Weinbaum as a little girl.

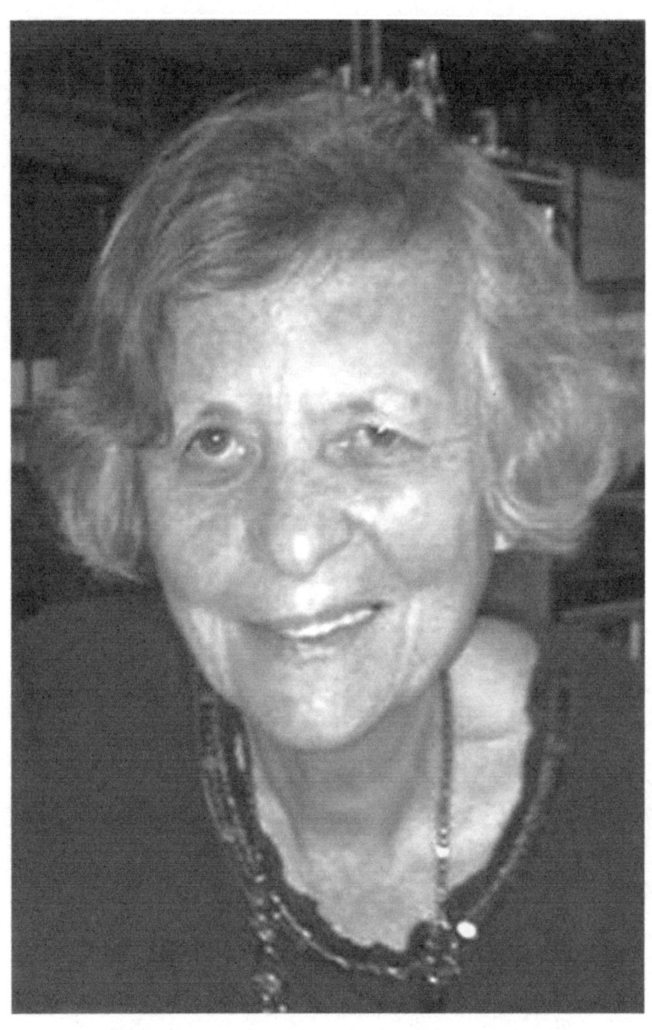

Steffi Weinbaum, today.

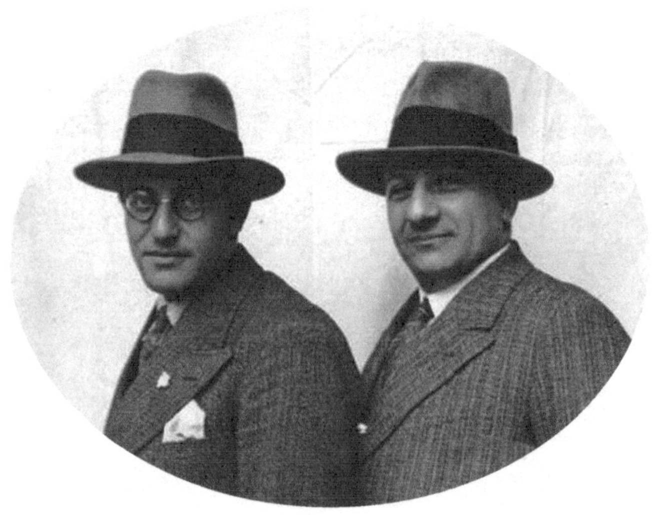

David's father and uncle Nathan.

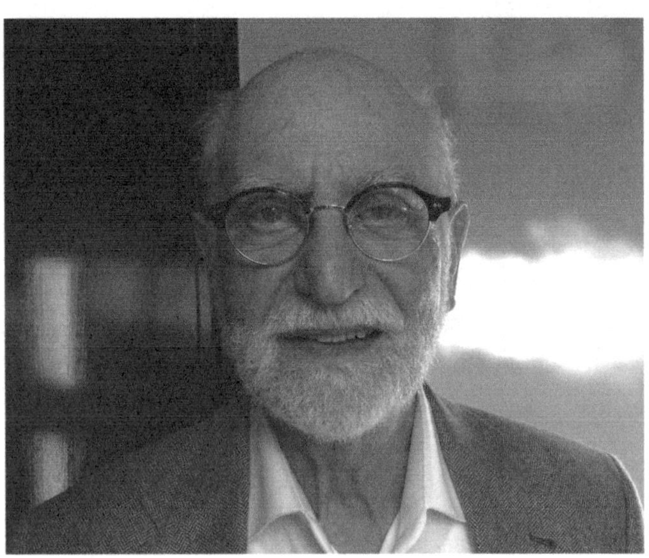

David Cohen, at eighty.

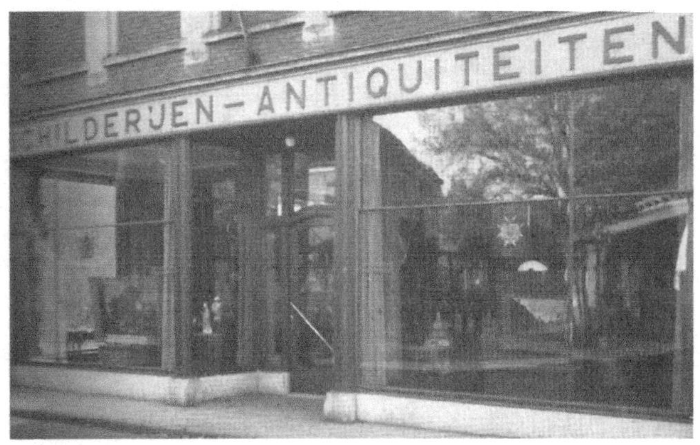

The store in Dieren.

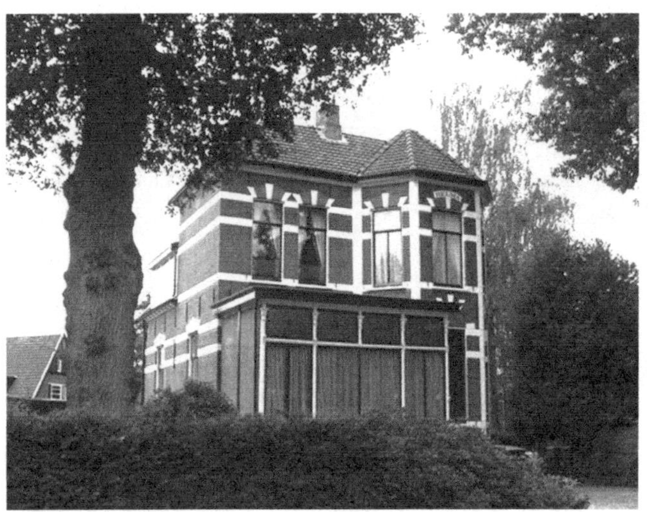

The villa in Dieren.

Works Cited

Aalders, Gerard, *Berooid, de beroofde joden en het Nederlands restitutiebeleid*, Uitgeverij Boom, Amsterdam, 2001.

Aalders, Gerard, *Roof, de ontvreemding van joods bezit tijdens de Tweede Wereldoorlog*, SDU Uitgevers, 1999.

Euwe, Jeroen, *De Nederlandse kunstmarkt 1940-1945*, Uitgeverij Boom, Amsterdam, 2007.

FüllbergStolberg, Klaus and Katja, *Jewish Exile in the British Colonial Empire –Gibraltar Camp, Jamaica, 1942-1947*, 1990 (?)

Hollander, Pieter den, *Roofkunst. De zaak Goudstikker,* Meulenhoff, Amsterdam, 2007.

Jong, dr. L. de, *Het koninkrijk der Nederlanden in de Tweede Wereldoorlog,* Part 5, March '4 1 July '42, second half, Martinus Nijhoff, 'sGravenhage, 1974.

Katz, Eva, Elsevier, tijdschrift, 1 december, 1973.

Kooger, Hans, *Joods Leven in Dieren, Rheden en Velp*, De Walburg Pers, Zutphen, 1987.

Schretlen, Helen, *Betwist bezit. De Stichting Nederlands Kunstbezit en de teruggave van roofkunst na 1945*, Waanders, Zwolle, 2002.

Tentoonstelling van 16e en 17e Eeuwse Hollandse, Vlaamse en Italiaanse Schilderijen, Commissie Waalbrug 1936, Nijmegen.

Tentoonstelling van 16e en 17e Eeuwse Hollandse en Vlaamse Schilderijen, in the rooms of the Arti et

Amicitiae Society, Amsterdam, from 7 May to 4 June 1938, Firma D. Katz, Dieren at Arnhem.
Venema, Adriaan, *Kunsthandel in Nederland, 1940-1945*, De Arbeiderspers Amsterdam, 1986.
http://dcclark.info.yorku.ca/files/2015/09/Dreams-of-Re-Creation-in-Jamaica-1.pdf?7fb97d, page 68 to 76.